2nd Workshop on Technologies for MT of Low Resource Languages (LoResMT 2019)

Held at Machine Translation Summit XVII

Dublin, Ireland
20 August 2019

ISBN: 978-1-5108-9246-0

Machine Translation Summit XVII

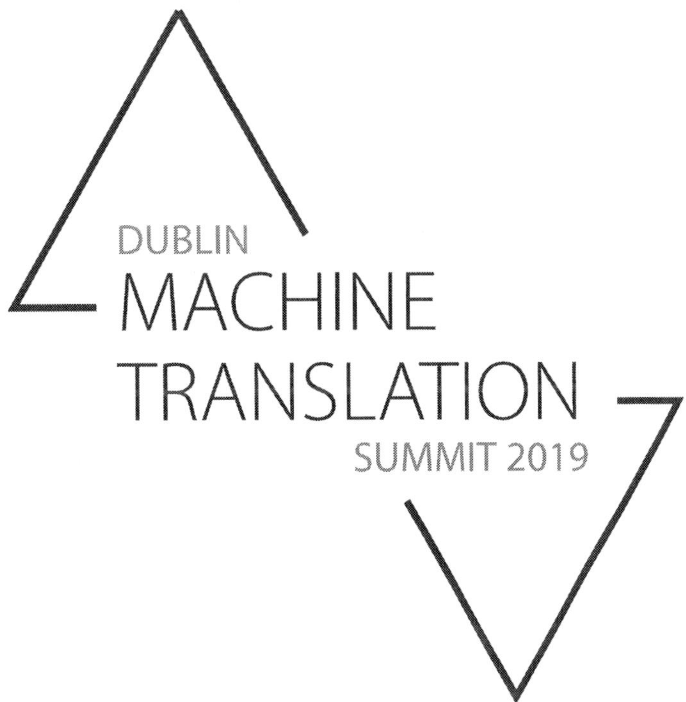

The 2nd Workshop on Technologies for MT of Low Resource Languages (LoResMT 2019)

https://sites.google.com/view/loresmt/

20 August, 2019
Dublin, Ireland

The 2nd Workshop on Technologies for MT of Low Resource Languages (LoResMT 2019)

https://sites.google.com/view/loresmt/

20 August, 2019
Dublin, Ireland

Preface from the co-chairs of the workshop

Machine translation (MT) technologies have been improved significantly in the last two decades, with the developments on phrased-based statistical MT (SMT) and recently the neural MT (NMT). However, most of these methods rely on the availability of large parallel data (millions to tens of millions sentence pairs) in the training, which are resources that do not exist in many language pairs. The development of monolingual MT is a recent approach that enables building MT systems without parallel data. However, a large amount of monolingual corpus is still required to train this kind of MT systems.

The workshop solicits papers on MT systems/methods for low resource languages in general. We hope to provide a forum for researchers working on MT for low resource languages and relevant NLP tools from our community. This year the LoResMT proceeding archives MT research on languages from all over the world, e.g. Crimean Tatar, Dravidian, Irish, Malayalam, Shipibo-Konibo, Torwali, Turkish. In addition, research on no-resource situation and the use of NMT for low resource languages will also be presented in LoResMT. Shared Tasks on MT for Bhojpuri, Magahi, Sindhi and Latvian (to and from English) is also organized under LoResMT, by Atul Kr. Ojha, Valentin Malykh, Pinkey Nainwani, Varvara Logacheva and Chao-Hong Liu. Two system description papers are archived in the proceeding.

In the LoResMT workshop, two corpus-building research teams will introduce their on-going work and resulting linguistic resources. They are DARPA LORELEI Program team led by Jennifer Tracey that curates corpora of low resource languages globally, and Minzu University of China team led by Xiaobing Zhao that builds corpora of minority languages in China, e.g. Mongolian, Tibetan and Uyghur. Researchers, led by Suo-nancairang, who work on the Tibetan language from Qinghai Normal University will also present their research at LoResMT.

We would like to express our sincere gratitude to the many researchers who helped as organizers, and reviewers and made the workshop successful. We are especially thankful to MT Summit organizers Andy Way, Antonio Toral, Jane Dunne for their continuous help on the workshop, and Alberto Poncelas for his various helps including the preparation of the proceeding. We are very grateful to the authors who submitted their work to the workshop and come to exchange their research at the venue. Thank you so much!

Chao-Hong Liu and Alina Karakanta

Organizers

Workshop Chairs

Alina Karakanta	Fondazione Bruno Kessler (FBK)
Atul Kr. Ojha	Panlingua Languague Processing LLP, New Delhi
Chao-Hong Liu	ADAPT Centre, Dublin City University
Jonathan Washington	Swarthmore College
Nathaniel Oco	National University (Phillippines)
Surafel Melaku Lakew	Fondazione Bruno Kessler (FBK)
Valentin Malykh	Huawei, Moscow Institute of Physics and Technology
Xiaobing Zhao	Minzu University of China

Program Committee

Alberto Poncelas	ADAPT Centre, Dublin City University
Alina Karakanta	Fondazione Bruno Kessler (FBK)
Atul Kr. Ojha	Panlingua Languague Processing LLP, New Delhi
Chao-Hong Liu	ADAPT Centre, Dublin City University
Daria Dzendzik	ADAPT Centre, Dublin City University
Eva Vanmassenhove	ADAPT Centre, Dublin City University
Koel Dutta Chowdhury	Saarland University
Majid Latifi	Universitat Politècnica de Catalunya
Meghan Dowling	ADAPT Centre, Dublin City University
Nathaniel Oco	National University (Phillippines)
Sangjee Dondrub	Qinghai Normal University
Santanu Pal	Saarland University
Surafel Melaku Lakew	Fondazione Bruno Kessler (FBK)
Tewodros Abebe	Addis Ababa University
Thepchai Supnithi	NECTEC
Valentin Malykh	Huawei, Moscow Institute of Physics and Technology
Vinit Ravishankar	University of Oslo
Yalemisew Abgaz	ADAPT Centre, Dublin City University

Contents

Finite State Transducer based Morphology analysis for Malayalam Language

Santhosh Thottingal

Swathanthra Malayalam Computing(smc.org.in)

Kerala, India

santhosh.thottingal@gmail.com

Abstract

This paper presents a finite state transducer approach to morphology analyser and generator for Malayalam language, an agglutinative, inflectional Dravidian language spoken by 38 million people, mainly by people from Kerala, India. This system, named as Mlmorph, is implemented using Stuttgart Finite State Transducer(SFST) formalism and uses Helsinki Finite-State Technology(HFST) as Toolkit. Evaluations show that it is fast and effective to address the morphological and phonological nature of Malayalam. Applications like spellchecker, named entity recognition, number spell out parser and generator are also built on top of Mlmorph.

1   Introduction

Malayalam is a language spoken in India, predominantly in the state of Kerala with about 38 million speakers. This Dravidian language has a rich morphology characterized by inflection and agglutination. Addressing this morphology is a prerequisite for any progress in language computing. Even though there were several efforts on this front, there is no functional morphology analyser for Malayalam. The Malayalam morphology analyser, named as **Mlmorph** presented in this paper tries to solve this. This paper first explains the nature of Malayalam morphology briefly. Then

the methodology of morphology analyser and implementation is explained in detail. Evaluation method and results are discussed at the end. A brief description of some of the applications already built on top of this analyser is a lso provided.

2   Malayalam

Malayalam is a heavily agglutinated and inflected language(Asher, 2013). The words are formed by the morphological processes involving (a) *Inflection* where a word in a lexical category undergoes inflection by attaching suffixes to it, generating a new word in the same category (b) *Derivation* where a word belonging to a category becomes another category by attaching a suffix, (c) *Compounding* where a new word is formed by combining two or more nouns, noun and adjective, adjective and noun, verb and noun, or adverb and verb.

2.1   Morphology of nouns

Nouns get inflected due to gender, number or cases(nominative, accusative, dative, sociative, instrumental, genitive and locative). Some examples:

1. പൂച്ചകൾ → പൂച്ച<n><pl>
    cats   → *cat<n><pl>*

2. ഇലയിൽ → ഇല<n><locative>
    on leaf → *leaf<n><locative>*

Adjectives can be derived from nouns, changing the root word suffix. An adjective can get agglutinated with a noun as given below.

പണപ്പെട്ടിയിൽ→ പണം<n><adj> + പെട്ടി <n><locative>

in money box → money<n><adj> + box <n><locative>

The above example also illustrate that derivation, agglutination, inflection - all these three can happen in a single word. Also, they can happen more than once in a single word. Example:

പഞ്ചസാരമണൽത്തരികളിലുമാണ് →
പഞ്ചസാര<n><adj> + മണൽ<n><adj> + തരി<n><pl><locative> + ഉം<cnj> + ആണ്<aff> *it is in the sugar-white grainy sands too → sugar<n><adj> + sand<n><adj> + grain<n><pl><locative> + too<cnj> + is<aff>*

2.2 Morphology of verbs

Verbs in Malayalam get inflected based on tense, mood, voice and aspect(Varma, 2006). Verbs are inflected for present, past and future tenses. Perfect, habitual and iterative aspects are very common. Iterative aspect has tense and emphatic variations. Verbs get inflected with causative and passive voices as well. A variety of mood forms such as abilitative, imperative, compulsive, promissive, optative, purposive, permissive, precative, irrealis, monitory, conditional, satisfactive exist. All of these forms are supported by Mlmorph. Some examples are given below.

ചിരിച്ചു → ചിരിക്കുക<v><past>
laughed → laugh<v><past>

ചിരിച്ചുകൊണ്ടിരുന്ന → ചിരിക്കുക<v> <iterative-past-aspect><adv-clause-rp-past>
the one who kept laughing → laugh <v><iterative-past-aspect><adv-clause-rp-past>

Nouns can be derived from verbs and then it can undergo all nominal inflections or agglutinations.

പാടിക്കൊണ്ടിരിക്കൽ → പാട്ടുക<v><iterative-aspect><n><deriv>
continuous singing → sing<v><iterative-aspect><n><deriv>

3 Methodology

Mlmorph is based on Finite State Transducer technology. A finite state transducer (FST) maps strings from one regular language (surface language) onto strings from another regular language (analysis language). This process is reversible too. The same transducer can be used to generate (i) analyses for a surface form (in analysis mode) and (ii) surface forms for an analysis (in generation mode). The number of generated or analysed output strings is usually one, but can be more than one while handling morphology variations specific to a language.

3.1 Implementation

The Mlmorph is written in the SFST transducer specification language which is based on extended regular expressions with variables and operators for concatenation, conjunction, disjunction, repetition, composition, negation, context-dependent replacement, and more(Schmid, 2005). A compiler translates the transducer specifications to an optimal automata. The generator automata can be reversed to create the analyser automata using the same compiler. For Mlmorph, the SFST based morphology model is compiled using Helsinki Finite-State Technology(HFST) toolkit (Lindén et al., 2011). HFST provides programming language interfaces such as python binding, and several tools to work with the compiled automata. SFST is one of the backends HFST supports.

Mlmorph has the following top level composition.

```
$analysis−filter$ || $morph$ || $phon$
   || $delete−pos$
```

This composition results in a morphology generator. Reversing the order of composition, we get analyser. First, the analysis symbols are passed through a filter `$analysis-filter$`. It accepts only the known characters and tags for Mlmorph. It then goes through the morphology rules defined by `$morph$`. The results of morphology generation is applied with the phonological rules defined by `$phon$`. Finally, all POS tags and intermediate tags used internally are removed using `$delete-pos$`. The output is the generated word.

In the transducer `$morph$`, we define what is a word model for Malayalam - `$word$`. We define it is a union of nouns(`$nouns$`), verbs(`$verbs$`), adjectives, adverbs, interjection, quantifiers etc. Kleene's plus(+) and star(*) operators has their usual meaning to denote number of occurrences.

```
$word$ = $punctuations$? ( $nouns$ \
```

| $verb$ | $noun_verb_compounds$ \
| $adjective$+ | $adverb$+ \
...
)? $punctuations$*

For the sake of brevity, we will explain noun and verb transducer here. A noun is formed by a union of singular nouns or plural nouns. A demonstrative(dem) or adjective($adjective$) can precede it. The nominal inflectional forms [#ninfl#], postpositions, conjuctions, polarity forms, quantifiers etc. can be suffixes. The whole word then goes through the nominal inflection rules defined by $ninfl$ transducer.

```
$suffixes$ = $postpositions$ |
    $conjunction$ | $polarity$ |
    $quantifiers$
$noun$ = $dem$ | ( $dem$? $adjective$? (
    $singular_noun$ | $plural_noun$ )
[#ninfl#]? $suffixes$? ) || $ninfl$
```

The verb model is defined as a verb stem from the defined lexicon going through a composition of union of tense, mood, aspect and adverb forms of verbal inflection.

```
$verb$ = $vstem$ || ( $verb−tenses$ |
    $verb−moods$ | $verb−aspects$ |
    $verb−adverbs$ )
```

The phonological transducer $phon$ applies the composition of phonological rules on the results of previous steps. The changes are mainly based on the last letter of first joining morpheme and first letter of second morpheme.

A python library is implemented on top of the automata generated[1], that abstracts analysis and generation, making Mlmorph easy to use in other applications. A web interface is also available to try out[2]. It also provides web APIs for other applications to consume.

3.2 Lexicon

The lexicon of Mlmorph contains the root words, classified and tagged into the following categories: nouns, person names, place names, postpositions, pronouns, quantifiers, abbreviations, adjectives, verbs, adverb, affirmatives, conjunctions, demonstratives, English borrowed nouns, Sanskrit rooted nouns, interjections and language names.

This lexicon is sourced from Malayalam Wiktionary, Wikipedia(based on categories there), CLDR(for language, place names) etc. The collected words are manually proofread and cleaned up. This task is tedious, but is very critical to the quality of analysis. It is also observed that the coverage ratio of Mlmorph largely depends on lexicon size.

3.3 POS tags

There is no agreement or standard on the POS tagging schema to be used for Malayalam. The general disagreement is about naming, which is very trivial to fix using a tag name mapper. The other issue is classification of features, which I found that there no elaborate schema that can cover Malayalam. So Mlmorph uses its own POS tagging schema and wherever possible the POS tags from Universal dependencies[3] (McDonald et al., 2013) are used. So far Mlmorph has defined 87 POS tags.

4 Applications

A morphology analyser and generator is the foundation for many language computing applications. As we have a functional morphology analyser now, a few applications were built on top of it, mainly to showcase some use cases.

4.1 Malayalam number spell out

In Malayalam, the spell out of numbers forms a single word. For example, a number 108 is നൂറ്റെട്ട് – a single word. This word is formed by adjective form of നൂറ്(100) with എട്ട്(8). While these two words are glued, Malayalam phonological rules are also applied, resulting compounded word നൂറ്റെട്ട്. Parsing the number നൂറ്റെട്ട് and interpreting it as 108 or converting 108 to നൂറ്റെട്ട് is an interesting problem in Malayalam computing.(Thottingal, 2017).

4.2 Spelling checker

The productive morphology of Malayalam causes practically infinite vocabulary. So a word list based approach for spellcheck won't work. A morphology analyser based spellchecker was developed and found to be effective in addressing this long pending need for the language(Thottingal, 2018). A word is correctly spelled if the word can be analysed using

---

[1] https://pypi.org/project/mlmorph/
[2] https://morph.smc.org.in/

[3] http://universaldependencies.org/

morphology analyser. If not, a variety of correction strategies were applied to find spelling correction candidates.

4.3 Named entity recognition

Identifying the named entities in words that are inflected or agglutinated was a challenge, but with the morphology analyser it is now possible to easily identify them by analysing each words. It is also possible to get better search results for named entities like people names, person names or places in large text for content using the same approach. (Thottingal, 2019).

5 Evaluation and Results

The evaluation of the system is done in three levels:

1. The Mlmorph is developed in a test driven approach. A manually prepared test case containing a word and its morphology analysis is first added to the collection of test cases. Then the analyser is enhanced to pass this test while not breaking any other tests that are already existing. About 450 such tests are present in the system. The same tests are used for morphology generator. So every analysis in the test case should generate the word by passing through the morphology generator. The test success rate is 100%

2. A set of 50,000 Malayalam words from the Malayalam corpus project of SMC[4] were used for the coverage analysis. The content in this set is already proofread and cleaned up to avoid words from other languages. It was found that 84% of words are analysed by Mlmorph. For the words that are not able to parse by the analyser, a frequency analysis is done, and top items in that list are considered for the tests in first level.

3. 1.4 million words collection, from all articles of Malayalam Wikipedia as of January 1, 2019 is used for testing. It can have spelling mistakes, words and acronyms from other languages like English. Also it can have many named entities that are not present in the lexicon of

Mlmorph compared to the processed corpus in previous step of evaluation. The current coverage for this corpus is 45%.

5.1 Performance

The Mlmorph implementation is reasonably fast as illustrated in Table 1. There is a constant time delay to load the whole automata of 12MB to memory and get ready for processing words. The time given in Table 1 includes that. The performance of the applications are very similar to this.

Number of words	Time taken for analysis
800	2 seconds
40,000	5 seconds
1400000	90 seconds

Table 1: Performance of Mlmorph. System: 64bit 4×i7-7600U CPU @ 2.80GHz, 15GB RAM

6 Future work

From the evaluation, it was observed that most of the words that the analyser failed to analyse are less frequent, but valid named entities such as person names, place names, brand names, language names etc. Adding more such words to lexicon is a never ending task, but having a better coverage based on large corpus evaluation, the effectiveness of Mlmorph can be enhanced. A few automated lexicon enhancements and possible sources for such words are being actively explored.

7 Concluding remarks

This paper presented the first functional system for Malayalam morphology. The transducer has addressed the agglutinational and inflectional properties of Malayalam. The system has the potential to be of an important component of language computing tools such as spell checker, search, named entity recognition and machine translation. The code is available under a free/open-source license(MIT license)[5]. The analyser, generator, named entity recognition applications are available at project website[6].

---

[4] https://gitlab.com/smc/corpus

[5] https://gitlab.com/smc/mlmorph
[6] https://morph.smc.org.in

References

Asher, Ronald E. 2013. *Malayalam*. Routledge.

Lindén, Krister, Erik Axelson, Sam Hardwick, Tommi A Pirinen, and Miikka Silfverberg. 2011. Hfst—framework for compiling and applying morphologies. In *International Workshop on Systems and Frameworks for Computational Morphology*, pages 67–85. Springer.

McDonald, Ryan, Joakim Nivre, Yvonne Quirmbach-Brundage, Yoav Goldberg, Dipanjan Das, Kuzman Ganchev, Keith Hall, Slav Petrov, Hao Zhang, Oscar Täckström, et al. 2013. Universal dependency annotation for multilingual parsing. In *Proceedings of the 51st Annual Meeting of the Association for Computational Linguistics (Volume 2: Short Papers)*, volume 2, pages 92–97.

Schmid, Helmut. 2005. A programming language for finite state transducers. In *FSMNLP*, volume 4002, pages 308–309.

Thottingal, Santhosh. 2017. Number spellout and generation in malayalam using morphology analyser. http://thottingal.in/blog/2017/12/10/number-spellout-and-generation-in-malayalam-using-morphology-analyser/. Accessed: 2019-05-15.

Thottingal, Santhosh. 2018. Malayalam spellchecker – a morphology analyser based approach. https://thottingal.in/blog/2018/09/08/malayalam-spellchecker-a-morphology-analyser-based-approach/. Accessed: 2019-05-15.

Thottingal, Santhosh. 2019. Malayalam named entity recognition using morphology analyser. https://thottingal.in/blog/2019/03/10/malayalam-named-entity-recognition-using-morphology-analyser/. Accessed: 2019-05-15.

Varma, AR Rajaraja. 2006. *Keralapanineeyam*. DC books, 8 edition.

A step towards Torwali machine translation: an analysis of morphosyntactic challenges in a low-resource language

Naeem Uddin
Torwali Research Forum
naeemuddinhadi@gmail.com

Jalal Uddin
Torwali Research Forum
torwalipk@gmail.com

Abstract

Torwali is an endangered language spoken in the north of Pakistan. It is a computationally challenging language because of its RTL Perso-Arabic script, non-concatenative nature and distinct words alterations. This paper discusses issues and challenges regarding grammatical structure, divergence in terms of lexicon as well as morphological make-up for the machine translation of a less studied language. It includes creation of NLP tools such as parts of speech (POS) tagger and morphological analyser with HFST which is based on the idea of building lexicon and morphological rules using finite state devices. This work, on which this paper is based, will be a source of Torwali finite state morphology and its future computational growth as electronic dictionaries are usually equipped with morphological analyser and it will also be helpful for developing language pairs.

Key words: Machine Translation, Low-resource language, Morphological analysis, language pairs

1   Introduction

Torwali belongs to the Kohistani sub-group of the Indo-Aryan Dardic languages, spoken in the upper reaches of district Swat of northern Pakistan. It has two dialects (the Bahrain and Chail dialects), with a total of approximately 90,000 to 100,000 speakers.

Torwali is written in a cursive, context sensitive Perso-Arabic script from left to right having unique grammar (morphology + syntax). Being a marginalized and low resource language, there are no robust morphology sources which hinders progress in NLP (Natural Language Processing) tools for Torwali thou there is a digital Torwali dictionary available along with some structured data. This paper discusses an attempt to create a morphological analyzer using HFST from scratch.

In NLP, morphological analysis is used to identify the morpheme and affixes of words in a language and individual words are analyzed into their components. Apart from computational linguistics, there are other uses that require morphological analysis e.g text processing, information retrieval and user interfaces.

Morphologies nowadays are commonly written by using special purpose languages based on finite state technology, one of them is HFST which is based on regular expressions.

2   Goals

The goal of this study is to create a baseline system that paves way for machine translation of Torwali which will cover:

- POS tagging
- Creating a lexc
- Basic inflection rules using twol (two level rule)

3   Unicode and input method

Unicode UTF-8 encoding is used as an encoding scheme as XFST/HFST files are always treated as UTF-8.

As an Input tool TRF phonetic keyboard (TRF 2L V1.0) is used which is developed so that users can easily input texts without going on-screen.

4   Morphological analysis using HFST

HFST-Helsinki finite-state Technology is a framework for compiling and applying linguistic descriptions with finite state methods. Finite-state transducers methods are useful for solving problems involving language identification via morphological processing and POS tagging. There are two principle files in a morphological transducer in HFST, a lexc file which is concerned with morphotactics i-e about the way morphemes are joined together in a word and twol file is used to describe phonological and orthographical alternation rules i-e about what happened when the morphemes are joined together.

For morphological analysis of Torwali HFST/finite state transducers are chosen because Torwali language is quite immature for statistical machine translation and also this implementation is done using Apertium, which is an open source machine translation platform in which HFST can be used.

4.1 LEXC

Lexicon Compiler or LEXC is a finite-state compiler also called a lexical transducer that reads set of morphemes and their morphotactic combinations in order to create finite-state transducer of a lexicon. LEXC contains morphemes grouped in sub-lexicon sets which in turn contain finite strings separated by ':' and a continuation class (a lexicon name).

4.2 TWOLC

TWOLC, **Two-Level Compiler** is a two level rule compiler used for compiling grammars of two levels into finite state transducers sets. Two level rules are constraints on lexical word forms corresponding to surface forms, It describes morphological alternations such as ژینگو:ژینگ (*weep: weeping*), بنو:بن (*say: saying*). It takes surface forms produced by LEXC and applies rules on them; the rules vary depending on morphological alteration of stem, morphologically or phonologically conditioned deletion of suffix, morphologically or phonologically conditioned insertion, morphologically or phonologically conditioned symbol change.

5   Torwali Morphology

Torwali has a unique morphology because it is basically a fusional language which uses several strategies like stem modification, reduplication and existence of words in inflected form, derived form, compound form and root form. The morphological analyzer separates root and suffix morphemes in all lexical entries i-e in أميزيل and لناچا ,الن/ ,أميز/ are roots and يل/,چا/ are suffixes. The purpose of this section is to discuss Torwali morphology and its implementation in HFST for main grammatical categories of Torwali i-e nouns, verbs, adjectives and pronouns.

5.1   Nouns

In Torwali, nouns are inflected for number and case and the stem can be joined by an optional plural suffix and an optional oblique case marker. Torwali uses several strategies to mark plurality but the primary morphological method is tone along with verb agreement like for most of the singular nouns have a tone with rising pitch from low-to-high and their plural counterparts have a tone with low pitch. Due to the issue related to representing tone, Torwali words which use tone to mark plurality the following approach is used where singular/plural for masculine and feminine are handled in a single paradigm.

Table 1: tags

tag	description
N-M	Noun masculine
N-F	Noun feminine
N-MF	Noun masculine/feminine

```
Multichar_Symbols
! Part of speech categories
%<n%>       ! Noun

! Number morphology
%<pl%>  ! Plural
%<sg%>  ! Singular

! Gender
%<m%>   ! Masculine
%<f%>   ! Feminine

LEXICON Root
        NounRoot ;
LEXICON N-M
%<n%>%<m%>%<sg%>: # ;
%<n%>%<m%>%<pl%>: # ;
LEXICON N-F
 %<n%>%<f%>%<sg%>: # ;
 %<n%>%<m%>%<pl%>: # ;
```

And, words are added in the lexicon in the following way:

```
LEXICON NounRoot

    آن:آن N-M ;
    أر:أر N-F ;
```

If we compile the lexicon with `hfst-lexc` and test it with `hfst-fst2strings`, it spits out the following result:

```
آن:آن<n><m><sg>
آن:آن<n><m><pl>
أر:أر<n><f><sg>
أر:آن<n><f><pl>
```

The above output marks singularity and plurality for words having tonal change but have no description about the tone's pitch. To make plural oblique of nouns a suffix /e/, /ے/ is added to the stem as in the words; /شان/, /خار/ /خارے/ and /شان/, /شانے/.

Reduplication is another strategy to communicate plurality and intensity but not in the same way as tone does. For instance, /میل گیل/, /گال مال/, /اچی می/, /پہٹ پہٹ/, /چُن چُن/.

Torwali noun forms can be derived from adjectives which can be implemented by adding the suffix /اچا/ making noun root follow a continuation class:

```
%<%n>%<nder%>%<m%>:%>اچا # ;
%<%n>%<nder%>%<f%>:%>اچا # ;
```

Where `%<nder%>` is tag for derived noun.

For noun inflection which undergoes stem modifications, there is a lot of complexity regarding standard rule formation for them; here is a general conclusion:

For majority of masculine nouns the vowel changes form \a\ to \ə\ and for feminine nouns \a\ to \æ\ but some masculine and feminine nouns behave differently. For morphological alteration of the stem the following rules must be implemented using twolc, taking the surface forms produced by lexc.

- Delete (a,ا) for making plurals of masculine singular nouns, when (a,ا) follows a consonant as in /ژن/, /ژان/ and /دن/, /ناد/
- Replace (a,ا) by (æ,أ) for making plurals of feminine nouns when the (a,ا) follows a consonant as in /بات/, /بأت/ and /ژات/, /ژأت/ .
- For noun inflections relating sizes; replace (a,ا) by (æ,أ) to mark small size of large-size nouns e.g. /لہاڑ/, /لہاڑ/.

5.2   Verbs

Torwali verbs inflect for tense, aspect, mood and gender and most of the verb forms make gender and number distinction only, no distinction for person. Torwali has three tenses: present, past and future. The suffix /i/, /ی/ can be used to mark feminine singular forms and present tense on feminine singular forms, /u/, /و/ as masculine singular suffix and present tense on masculine singular forms with the suffix /i/, /ی/ being used for present tense on plural forms too. For infinite verbs the suffix /u/ is added to the stem.

To make a test, only present tense on masculine and feminine, infinitives, transitive and intransitive forms of verb are selected and in the continuation class the suffixes are added to mark inflection associated with each of them which are defined with suitable tags as shown below.

```
Multichar_Symbols
! Part of speech categories
%<v%>        ! Verb

! Number morphology
%<pl%>   ! Plural
%<sg%>   ! Singular

! Gender
%<m%>    ! Masculine
%<f%>    ! Feminine

! Verb forms
%<pres%>  ! Pres
%<inf%>   ! Infinitives
%<vt%>    ! Verb Transitive
%<vi%>    ! Verb Intransitive
! Other symbols
%>        ! Morpheme boundary

LEXICON Root
          Verbs ;

  LEXICON V-INF
  %<v%>%<inf%>:%>و # ;
  %<v%>%<m%>%<pres%>:%>دو # ;
  %<v%>%<f%>%<pres%>:%>جی # ;
  LEXICON VT
  %<v%>%<vt%>:%>وؐ # ;
  LEXICON VI
  %<v%>%<vi%>:%>ہوؐ # ;
```

Now if we add some verbs,
```
LEXICON Verbs
ژینگ:ژینگ V ;
بن:بن V-INF ;
سُلو:سُلو VT ;
سُورَی:سُورَی VI ;
```

The analyzer analyses these verb forms in the following way when compiled with `hfst-lexc` and tested with `hfst-fst2strings`:

```
$ hfst-fst2strings trw.lexc.hfst

ژینگ<v>:ژینگ
و<بن<v><inf>:بن
دو<بن<v><m><pres>:بن
جی<بن<v><f><pres>:بن
وَ< سْلُو<v><vt>:سْلُو
بوؤ< سُورَئ<v><vi>:سُورَئ
```

From the above output it is concluded that the following implementations can be done. These rules can be applied to verbs whose stem ends with a consonant.

- Adding a suffix / دُد/ to represent past tense on infinitive verb.
- Adding a suffix /نین/ to mark future tense on finite verb.
- Adding suffix /سأت/ to mark inceptive of infinite verb.
- For present perfective on masculine singular adding suffix /و/ and /ئ/ for both plurals and feminine singular.
- Suffix /ودو/ for masculine singular, / یجی/ for feminine singular and /یدی/ for plurals to mark present perfective on finite verbs
- Suffix /وشو/ for masculine singular and /یشی/ for both feminine singular and plurals to mark past perfective on finite verb.

Verbs ending with a vowel inflect differently they sometimes behave like verbs with consonant ending stems with a minor modification some plural forms tend to have /ﺍٰ/with the stem before applying the plural suffix; however most of the verbs with vowel-final stem follow different configurations.

5.3 Adjectives, Pronouns, Adverbs and closed classes

In a similar way Adjectives, Pronouns, Adverbs, Postpositions, Conjunctions and Interjections have been implemented with the same level of detail.

6 Result and Conclusions

This work presents a straight forward implementation of Towali morphology analyzer using HFST, which implemented the basic inflections of nouns, verbs and other POS like adjectives, adverbs, pronouns and postpositions being tagged. We found HFST a good choice for implementing Torwali Morphology for now as this is the first ever attempt to implement Torwali morphology using FST. However; to develop a full fledge Morphological analyzer more work has to be done. The major problem which we have to face is the random stem changes in nouns, variation in nouns using change of tone, distinct behavior of vowel ending verbs and nouns. There is a need to learn more about Torwali Morphology regarding the affixes and varying stems and more rules needs to be defined.

7 Future work

This work could further be enhanced to following extensions depending upon the possibility:

- Addition of missing diacritic marks to words
- Technique to interpret tone of nouns to indentify singular/plural nouns by its tone.
- Algorithms to differentiate phonetically similar words.
- A comprehensive implementation of Torwali syntax.

8 References

Beesley, K.R, Karttunen, L.: Finite State Morphology. CSLI Publications, Palo Alto (2003)

K. Lindén, A. Erik, H. Sam, A. P. Tommi, and S. Miikka, "*HFST-Framework for Compiling and Applying Morphologies.*" International Workshop on Systems and Frameworks for Computational Morphology, Springer Berlin Heidelberg, 2011.

K. Linden, E. Axelson , S. Drobac, S. Hardwick, J. Kuokkala, J. Niemi, T. Pirinen and Silfverberg "*HFST—A System for Creating NLP Tools.*", International Workshop on Systems and Frameworks for Computational Morphology, Springer Berlin Heidelberg, 2013.

Ullah, Inam (2019) "Digital Dictionary Development for Torwali, A Less-studied Language: Process and Challenges," *Proceedings of the Workshop on Computational Methods for Endangered Languages*: Vol. 2 , Article 3.

Grierson, George A. 1929. *Torwali: An Account of a Dardic Language of the Swat Kohistan*. Royal Asiatic Society. London.

K. Linden, M. Silfverberg, , T. Pirinen, "HFST Tools for Morphology—An Efficient Open Source Package for Construction of Morphological Analyzers", In: Mahlow, Piotrowski (eds.) , pp. 28–47,2009.

Lunsford, Wayne. 2001. *An Overview of Linguistic Structures in Torwali, A Language of Northern Pakistan. M.A. Thesis, University of Texas at Arlington.*

Ullah, Inam. 2004. *'Lexical Database of the Torwali Dictionary.' In The Asia lexicography conference. Chiangmai: Payap University.*

Workflows for kickstarting RBMT in virtually No-Resource Situation

Tommi A Pirinen
Universität Hamburg,
Hamburger Zentrum für Sprachkorpora
Max-Brauer-Allee 60, Hamburg
tommi.antero.pirinen@uni-hamburg.de

Abstract

In this article we describe a work-in-progress best learnt practices on how to start working on rule-based machine translation when working with language that has virtually no pre-existing digital resources for NLP use. We use Karelian language as a case study, in the beginning of our project there were no publically available corpora, parallel or monolingual analysed, no analysers and no translation tools or language models. We show workflows that we have find useful to curate and develop necessary NLP resources for the language. Our workflow is aimed also for no-resources working in a sense of no funding and scarce access to native informants, we show that building core NLP resources in parallel can alleviate the problems therein.

1 Introduction

A lot of research goes into working with low-resource situation, however, in context of large international conferences today, loww-resources can mean anything from having millions and millions of lines of parallel corpus[1] to "anything except English". For this work we consider the lowest-resourced languages in the group of languages we work with, namely those having virtually no widely known publicly accessible or available resources at the start of

[1]http://www.statmt.org/wmt19/
parallel-corpus-filtering.html

our project, and for which we aim to search, curate and create the necessary resources. This is a work-in-progress, but we believe we have already gathered enough promising results to give some best recommended practices on how to start working on a language seemingly lacking all natural language processing (NLP) resources.

For the machine translation part we are working on doing a rule-based machine translation (RBMT) and specifically one between a minority language (Karelian) and a closely related more-resourced language (Finnish), in the first phase. The translator is bidirectional, i.e. we translate both Finnish to Karelian and vice versa. The work for majority language machine translations (e.g. English and Russian) is reserved for the future after some resources have been built. We have chosen this for a number of reasons, firstly the task is much easier when working with a related language than a typologically unrelated one, and secondly there is a body of good results using RBMT of closely related in further resource building, for example for Spanish-related languages in the Wikipedia content translation.

The article is organised as follows, first in Section 2 we describe the background and rationale for this project, in Section 3 we describe our approach and methodology for RBMT building, in Section 4 we describe our results so far and finally in the Section 5 we discuss findings and lay out future work.

2 Background

One of the problems, we have identified in the past in building NLP resources for minority languages, is that same or similar work ends up doing multiple times between different scholars, or even within a single project of same minority language. This is not very ideal situation, when resources like native informants or skilled scholars are scarce. A typical example might be that a documentary linguistics effort builds a corpus of annotated texts, that includes hand annotated linguistic analysis, glosses and translations, while computational linguists build a morphological analyser, treebank and machine translator by hand from scratch as well. What we aim to achieve is synergy between these two different research practices.

The technological methodology used in this project is based on following:

- The rule-based machine translation is provided by apertium (Forcada et al., 2011).

- The morphological analyser-generator is based on the HFST engine (Lindén et al., 2009)

- The morphological disambiguation is based on Constraint Grammar (Karlsson, 1990)

- annotation format is based on Universal dependencies (Nivre et al., 2019)

This article describes what is still a work-in-progress, at this stage we are evaluating how the approach is and if we should make a project in building the supporting software for the methodology and language resource building. That is to say we have the workflows in place and the supporting software is built as we proceed with the project. Some of the workflows described here have been previously tested in building larger well-resourced machine translators, for example in (Pirinen, 2018). Based on experiences of this project, we could estimate that the effort needed is around 20,000 lines annotated and translated to get a comparable results as out of the box neural system (Pirinen, 2019), this is however a result achieved on two unrelated languages both of which aren't English, so results on related non-English languages may be different.

We have selected to use a rule-based approach to machine-translation for this project. Since rule-based approaches have somewhat fallen out of popularity in recent years, it needs strong arguments to select this approach in favour of others. For this purpose we have a check-list for which languages are to be used with which approaches first:

- Closely related languages: Finnish and Karelian are very closely related languages

- Lack of Parallel resources: Karelian has virtually zero digital resources

- Existence of written grammars: We have number of grammars to help (Zaikov, 2013)

One of the reasons we started to develop an approach to language resource creation that can produce multiple language resources fast, is that we have prior experience in 1. building computational linguistic resources like morphological analysers from the scratch without considering the corpus creation or documentary linguistics and 2. building language documentation corpora from the scratch without considering creation of dictionaries. The ideal result of this project is to develop a method that empowers computational linguists to work on their preferred form of language documentation and corpus creation and makes use of the expert work put in. This can always be achieved afterhands by scraping the produced corpora or data, but our plan is to introduce that as a part of workflow.

For other projects that have aimed to achieve similar goals, many are related to other rule-based machine translation efforts within the free/open source rule-based machine translation community, e.g.(?). On larger scale in the NLP community there have been several attempts to make computational linguists and documentary linguists work together towards common goal in this manner, for example (Maxwell and David, 2008; Blokland et al., 2015)

The basis of this RBMT system between Karelian and Finnish is that we also have a large coverage stable Finnish system already available (Pirinen, 2015). Karelian on the other hand has no resources, and is described by the ethnologuy as threatened[2]. We could have also tested an unrelated language

---

[2]https://www.ethnologue.com/language/krl

with large coverage dictionary, for example
Russian-Karelian would be useful for the target audience, or build a machine translation
between two under-resourced closely related
languages, like Karelian and Livvi, which is
a closely related language with slightly more
resources than Karelian but much less than
Finnish.

Finally, for social and political reasons, there
is a growing interest in Karelian language and
culture, and while there is a number of projects
on the linguistic aspects and language learning,
there is a lack of language technology-based
projects in the field. Our aim is to fill that
hole.

2.1 Languages

The language we use a case study is Karelian, a
minority Uralic language spoken mainly in Republic of Karelia in Russia and in Finland. It
is closely related to Finnish, Livvi and Ludic,
but they are not mutually intelligible for an individual without at least some linguistic training. The naming of different languages and
varieties related to Karelian is often confusing,
what we aim to describe here is in line of ISO
639–3 language code krl; see the number 1 in
the map in Figure 1[3] for the geographic distribution. For the machine translation task, in
first phase we build a Karelian—Finnish translator.

3 Workflow

The workflow that we have reached at this
point of the project is a synthesis of traditional workflow in documentary linguistics and
workflows in building corpora and analyser
writing, specifically in traditional rule-based
systems. In documentational linguistics we
have drawn experience and inspiration from
SIL Fieldworks Explorer (FLeX) and the rule-based workflows are loosely based in tradition
of Finite State Morphology.

The first part of the workflow is acquiring corpora, which for unresourced minority
is relatively difficult task, at the beginning of
our project we aimed to use web-as-corpus approach. During categorising the downloaded
data into languages we found also a corpus

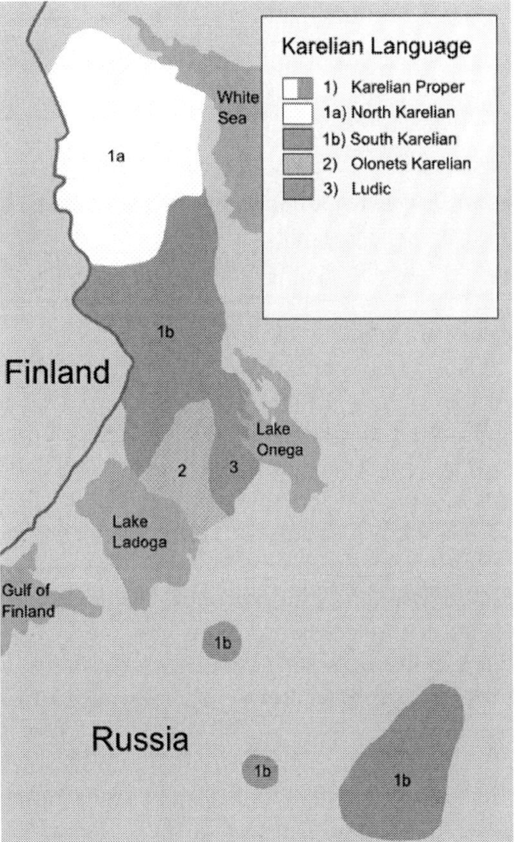

Figure 1: Map of Karelian languages, the number 1 is
Karelian that we study in this article, numbers 2 and
3 are closely related languages that are in some literature refered to as Karelian as well, but are separate
languages and do not belong under the krl language
code in ISO standard.

---

[3]https://commons.wikimedia.org/wiki/File:
Map_of_Karelian_dialects.png

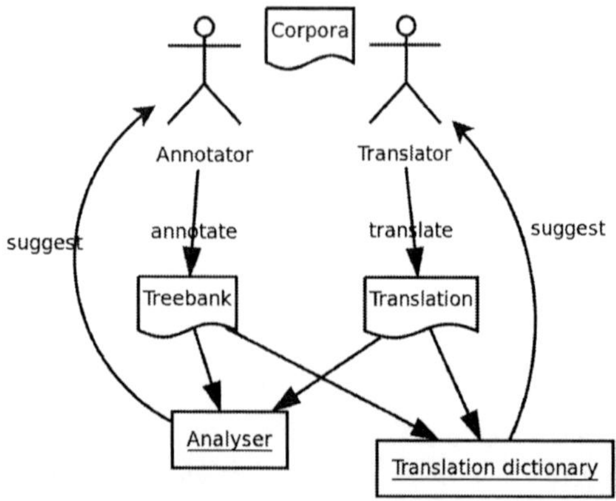

Figure 2: A UML-style chart of the annotation and translation process

repository with a free to use open source compatible licencing policy[4], which on top of expert made language classification has the advantage that we can keep full documents instead of shuffled sentences.

The actual corpus building workflow consists of two parts that can be alternated between, annotation and lexicon building. With annotation, we can work on any of the following tasks: lemmatising and pos tagging, morphological analysis, syntactic treebanking and machine translation. On the other side lexicon building we build the morphological lexicon for a finite-state analyser, and a bilingual lexicon for rule-based machine translation. A UML-style graph of the process is shown in figure 2.

The main contribution of this workflow is that both of the tasks feed into the other task, that is annotated corpora can be immediately used for entry generation of the lexicons, and the analysers and machine translators built from the lexicons are used to generate n-best lists from which annotators can choose the annotations.

We provide a real world example here: An annotator starts working on a new document that contains sentences: "Pelih ošallistu 13 henkie" (13 people participated in the play) the annotator annotates in UD format:

```
1 peliin peli  NOUN  Number=Sing|Case=Ill 2 obl _ _
2 ošallistu ošallistuo VERB  Number=Sing|Tense=Pres 0 root _ _
3 13 13 NUM Number=Sing|NumType=Card 4 nummod _ _
4 henkie henki NOUN  Number=Sing|Case=Par 2 nsubj _ _
```

and provides Finnish translation like "Peliin osallistui 13 henkilöä". The annotation is used to generate entries for monolingual dictionary of Karelian, i.e. peli<n>, ošallistuo<vblex>,

<hr>

[4] http://dictorpus.krc.karelia.ru/en/corpus/text

	Tokens	Sentences
Annotations	3094	228
Translations	1144	161

Table 1: The size of Karelian—Finnish corpus at the time of writing.

13<num>, and henki<n>, the lexicon writer can simply fill in the necessary informations to inflect the words properly. The entries can likewise be generated to bilingual dictionary, if 1:1 translation match to existing target language analyses is trivial, we get peli<n>:peli<n> etc. among the suggested entries. Now, when the annotator gets back to annotating and translating the next sentences of the document and runs into: "Pelissä "tapettih" šamoin Ilmarini" (Ilmarinen was also killed in the game), the first token "Pelissä" has suggested annotation peli NOUN Number=Sing|Case=Ine as well as suggested translation.

4 Results

In a short time we have managed to build a rule-based machine translation system. We detail the system in Table 1. The corpus built so far in this proto-typing phase of the project has been built by one expert annotator, working on spare time for three months in other words in only handful of work hours.

At the current moment we do not have enough bilingual corpora to measure the translation quality yet but we hope to include a BLEU and WER evaluations of the translation quality by the time we submit a camera-ready version of the paper.

The corpora will be released on github via the Apertium project for the translations and possibly also disambiguated corpora, and via Universal dependencies project for the annotated corpus. Both retain the CC BY licence of the original raw text data. The dictionaries and analysers are also released via the Apertium using the GNU General Public Licence.

5 Concluding remarks

We have found that we can rapidly build a solid base of natural language resourcses suitable for rule-based machine translation and we aim to extend the approach to more Uralic languages in near future. Furthermore the approach prototyped in this paper has been found very motivating and nice to work with in the future we will look at building a more approachable graphical user interface for it.

The approach we describe here is especially suitable in no-resources starting situation, even a limited amount of resources will open more workflows, more technical possibilities to aid in the initial part of the corpus building and resource building. However, we still think this approach may be useful as a part of balanced corpus building approach in a research project for any lesser researched language.

One of the things that we are looking forward to is to test the advances in neural methods in very low resource situation, (Neubig and Hu, 2018)[5] this would be particularly suitable for Karelian-to-Finnish direction as Finnish is well-resourced.

References

Blokland, Rogier, Marina Fedina, Ciprian Gerstenberger, Niko Partanen, Michael Rießler, and Joshua Wilbur. 2015. Language documentation meets language technology. In Septentrio Conference Series, number 2, pages 8–18.

Forcada, Mikel L, Mireia Ginestí-Rosell, Jacob Nordfalk, Jim O'Regan, Sergio Ortiz-Rojas, Juan Antonio Pérez-Ortiz, Felipe Sánchez-Martínez, Gema Ramírez-Sánchez, and Francis M Tyers. 2011. Apertium: a free/open-source platform for rule-based machine translation. Machine translation, 25(2):127–144.

Karlsson, Fred. 1990. Constraint grammar as a framework for parsing unrestricted text. In Karlgren, H., editor, Proceedings of the 13th International Conference of Computational Linguistics, volume 3, pages 168–173, Helsinki.

Lindén, Krister, Miikka Silfverberg, and Tommi Pirinen. 2009. Hfst tools for morphology—an efficient open-source package for construction of morphological analyzers. In Mahlow, Cerstin and Michael Piotrowski, editors, sfcm 2009, volume 41 of Lecture Notes in Computer Science, pages 28—47. Springer.

Maxwell, Michael and Anne David. 2008. Joint grammar development by linguists and computer scientists. In Workshop on NLP for Less Privileged Languages, Third International Joint Conference on Natural Language Processing, pages 27–34, Hyderabad, India.

Neubig, Graham and Junjie Hu. 2018. Rapid adaptation of neural machine translation to new languages. arXiv preprint arXiv:1808.04189.

Nivre, Joakim, Mitchell Abrams, Željko Agić, Lars Ahrenberg, Gabrielė Aleksandravičiūtė, Lene Antonsen, Katya Aplonova, Maria Jesus Aranzabe, Gashaw Arutie, Masayuki Asahara, Luma Ateyah, Mohammed Attia, Aitziber Atutxa, Liesbeth Augustinus, Elena Badmaeva, Miguel Ballesteros, Esha Banerjee, Sebastian Bank, Verginica Barbu Mititelu, Victoria Basmov, John Bauer, Sandra Bellato, Kepa Bengoetxea, Yevgeni Berzak, Irshad Ahmad Bhat, Riyaz Ahmad Bhat, Erica Biagetti, Eckhard Bick, Agnė Bielinskienė, Rogier Blokland, Victoria Bobicev, Loïc Boizou, Emanuel Borges Völker, Carl Börstell, Cristina Bosco, Gosse Bouma, Sam Bowman, Adriane Boyd, Kristina Brokaitė, Aljoscha Burchardt, Marie Candito, Bernard Caron, Gauthier Caron, Gülşen Cebiroğlu Eryiğit, Flavio Massimiliano Cecchini, Giuseppe G. A. Celano, Slavomír Čéplö, Savas Cetin, Fabricio Chalub, Jinho Choi, Yongseok Cho, Jayeol Chun, Silvie Cinková, Aurélie Collomb, Çağrı Çöltekin, Miriam Connor, Marine Courtin, Elizabeth Davidson, Marie-Catherine de Marneffe, Valeria de Paiva, Arantza Diaz de Ilarraza, Carly Dickerson, Bamba Dione, Peter Dirix, Kaja Dobrovoljc, Timothy Dozat, Kira Droganova, Puneet Dwivedi, Hanne Eckhoff, Marhaba Eli, Ali Elkahky, Binyam Ephrem, Tomaž Erjavec, Aline Etienne, Richárd Farkas, Hector Fernandez Alcalde, Jennifer Foster, Cláudia Freitas, Kazunori Fujita, Katarína Gajdošová, Daniel Galbraith, Marcos Garcia, Moa Gärdenfors, Sebastian Garza, Kim Gerdes, Filip Ginter, Iakes Goenaga, Koldo Gojenola, Memduh Gökırmak, Yoav Goldberg, Xavier Gómez Guinovart, Berta González Saavedra, Matias Grioni, Normunds Grūzītis, Bruno Guillaume, Céline Guillot-Barbance, Nizar Habash, Jan Hajič, Jan Hajič jr., Linh Hà Mỹ, Na-Rae Han, Kim Harris, Dag Haug, Johannes Heinecke, Felix Hennig, Barbora Hladká, Jaroslava Hlaváčová, Florinel Hociung, Petter Hohle, Jena Hwang, Takumi Ikeda, Radu Ion, Elena Irimia, Ọlájídé Ishola, Tomáš Jelínek, Anders Johannsen, Fredrik Jørgensen, Hüner Kaşıkara, Andre Kaasen, Sylvain Kahane, Hiroshi Kanayama, Jenna Kanerva, Boris Katz, Tolga Kayadelen, Jessica Kenney, Václava Kettnerová, Jesse Kirchner, Arne Köhn, Kamil Kopacewicz, Natalia Kotsyba, Jolanta Kovalevskaitė, Simon Krek, Sookyoung Kwak, Veronika Laippala, Lorenzo Lambertino, Lucia Lam, Tatiana Lando, Septina Dian Larasati, Alexei Lavrentiev, John Lee, Phương Lê Hồng, Alessandro Lenci, Saran Lertpradit, Herman

---

5 We thank the anonymous reviewers for bringing this line of work to our attention

Leung, Cheuk Ying Li, Josie Li, Keying Li, KyungTae Lim, Yuan Li, Nikola Ljubešić, Olga Loginova, Olga Lyashevskaya, Teresa Lynn, Vivien Macketanz, Aibek Makazhanov, Michael Mandl, Christopher Manning, Ruli Manurung, Cătălina Mărănduc, David Mareček, Katrin Marheinecke, Héctor Martínez Alonso, André Martins, Jan Mašek, Yuji Matsumoto, Ryan McDonald, Gustavo Mendonça, Niko Miekka, Margarita Misirpashayeva, Anna Missilä, Cătălin Mititelu, Yusuke Miyao, Simonetta Montemagni, Amir More, Laura Moreno Romero, Keiko Sophie Mori, Tomohiko Morioka, Shinsuke Mori, Shigeki Moro, Bjartur Mortensen, Bohdan Moskalevskyi, Kadri Muischnek, Yugo Murawaki, Kaili Müürisep, Pinkey Nainwani, Juan Ignacio Navarro Horñiacek, Anna Nedoluzhko, Gunta Nešpore-Bērzkalne, Lương Nguyễn Thị, Huyền Nguyễn Thị Minh, Yoshihiro Nikaido, Vitaly Nikolaev, Rattima Nitisaroj, Hanna Nurmi, Stina Ojala, Adédayọ̀ Olúòkun, Mai Omura, Petya Osenova, Robert Östling, Lilja Øvrelid, Niko Partanen, Elena Pascual, Marco Passarotti, Agnieszka Patejuk, Guilherme Paulino-Passos, Angelika Peljak-Łapińska, Siyao Peng, Cenel-Augusto Perez, Guy Perrier, Daria Petrova, Slav Petrov, Jussi Piitulainen, Tommi A Pirinen, Emily Pitler, Barbara Plank, Thierry Poibeau, Martin Popel, Lauma Pretkalnin̦a, Sophie Prévost, Prokopis Prokopidis, Adam Przepiórkowski, Tiina Puolakainen, Sampo Pyysalo, Andriela Rääbis, Alexandre Rademaker, Loganathan Ramasamy, Taraka Rama, Carlos Ramisch, Vinit Ravishankar, Livy Real, Siva Reddy, Georg Rehm, Michael Rießler, Erika Rimkutė, Larissa Rinaldi, Laura Rituma, Luisa Rocha, Mykhailo Romanenko, Rudolf Rosa, Davide Rovati, Valentin Roșca, Olga Rudina, Jack Rueter, Shoval Sadde, Benoît Sagot, Shadi Saleh, Alessio Salomoni, Tanja Samardžić, Stephanie Samson, Manuela Sanguinetti, Abigail Walsh Sarah McGuinness, Dage Särg, Baiba Saulīte, Yanin Sawanakunanon, Nathan Schneider, Sebastian Schuster, Djamé Seddah, Wolfgang Seeker, Mojgan Seraji, Mo Shen, Atsuko Shimada, Hiroyuki Shirasu, Muh Shohibussirri, Dmitry Sichinava, Natalia Silveira, Maria Simi, Radu Simionescu, Katalin Simkó, Mária Šimková, Kiril Simov, Aaron Smith, Isabela Soares-Bastos, Carolyn Spadine, Antonio Stella, Milan Straka, Jana Strnadová, Alane Suhr, Umut Sulubacak, Shingo Suzuki, Zsolt Szántó, Dima Taji, Yuta Takahashi, Fabio Tamburini, Takaaki Tanaka, Isabelle Tellier, Guillaume Thomas, Liisi Torga, Trond Trosterud, Anna Trukhina, Reut Tsarfaty, Francis Tyers, Sumire Uematsu, Zdeňka Urešová, Larraitz Uria, Hans Uszkoreit, Sowmya Vajjala, Daniel van Niekerk, Gertjan van Noord, Viktor Varga, Eric Villemonte de la Clergerie, Veronika Vincze, Lars Wallin, Jing Xian Wang, Jonathan North Washington, Maximilan Wendt, Seyi Williams, Mats Wirén, Christian Wittern, Tsegay Woldemariam, Tak-sum Wong, Alina Wróblewska, Mary Yako, Naoki Yamazaki, Chunxiao Yan, Koichi Yasuoka, Marat M. Yavrumyan, Zhuoran Yu, Zdeněk Žabokrtský, Amir Zeldes, Daniel Zeman, Manying Zhang, and Hanzhi Zhu. 2019. Universal dependencies 2.4. LINDAT/CLARIN digital library at the Institute of Formal and Applied Linguistics (ÚFAL), Faculty of Mathematics and Physics, Charles University.

Pirinen, Tommi A. 2015. Development and use of computational morphology of finnish in the open source and open science era: Notes on experiences with omorfi development. SKY Journal of Linguistics, 28.

Pirinen, Tommi A. 2018. Rule-based machine-translation between finnish and german.

Pirinen, Tommi A. 2019. Neural and rule-based finnish nlp models—expectations, experiments and experiences. In Proceedings of the Fifth International Workshop on Computational Linguistics for Uralic Languages, pages 104–114.

Zaikov, Pekka. 2013. Vienankarjalan kielioppi.

A Continuous Improvement Framework of Machine Translation for Shipibo-Konibo

Erasmo Gómez Montoya[✻]   Kervy Rivas-Rojas[✻]   Arturo Oncevay[✻♠]

[✻] Department of Engineering, Pontificia Universidad Católica del Perú
[♠] School of Informatics, University of Edinburgh
{hector.gomez,k.rivas}@pucp.pe, a.oncevay@ed.ac.uk

Abstract

Shipibo-Konibo is a low-resource language from Peru with prior results in statistical machine translation; however, it is challenging to enhance them mainly due to the expensiveness of building more parallel corpora. Thus, we aim for a continuous improvement framework of the Spanish–Shipibo-Konibo language-pair by taking advantage of more advanced strategies and crowd-sourcing. Besides the introduction of a new domain for translation based on language learning flashcards, our main contributions are the extension of the machine translation experiments for Shipibo-Konibo to neural architectures with transfer and active learning; and the building of a conversational agent prototype to retrieve new translations through a social media platform.

1 Introduction

The focus on low-resource Machine Translation (MT) has driven further work with different machine learning settings to take advantage of Neural MT (NMT) methods, where the amount of training data is relevant to obtain quality results (Koehn and Knowles, 2017). For instance, with a Transfer Learning approach, we can learn specific components in a system from a resource-rich domain (e.g. a language-pair) and transfer the updated parameters to the real target (Zoph et al., 2016), usually in a resource-poor domain. Regarding the size of available corpora, with Active Learning methods, we can rank new samples to label (e.g. sentences to translate) to improve a learning system efficiently (Haffari et al., 2009). Besides, crowd-sourcing strategies and platforms, such as Amazon Mechanical Turk, have gained attention in translation studies and MT to retrieve less expensive corpora (Jiménez-Crespo, 2017).

Given the background, Peru offers a diversity-rich language context for MT research with more than 40 native languages (Simons and Fenning, 2019) that are typologically different from Castilian Spanish (spa), the primary official language in the country. Specifically, Shipibo-Konibo (shp) is an Amazonian language that has been addressed in Natural Language Processing (NLP) recently, including a statistical MT (SMT) study with religious and educational domain corpora (Galarreta et al., 2017). However, the language is far from being considered a rich-resource one with less than 20,000 sentences for the spa–shp language-pair. Thus, it is crucial to look for different approaches that could deliver better MT systems, and also, new parallel corpus.

Therefore, this study extends previous MT studies of Shipibo-Konibo by introducing a new domain for translation based on flashcards for language learning (see §4), experimenting with transfer and active learning strategies in neural architectures (see §5), and proposing a conversational agent prototype in social media to retrieve new translations from native speakers (see §6). Our main goal is to mount an initial framework able to continuously improve MT for Peruvian languages, with the potential to include further NMT features. To complement the article, §2 presents previous work on MT for Peruvian languages, §3 introduces more details about the target language, and finally, §7 concludes and proposes further steps.

	$\mathcal{S}$	$\overline{r}_{\text{shp–spa}}$	$\mathcal{T}$		$|\mathcal{V}|$		HLT	
			spa	shp	spa	shp	spa	shp
Religious	12,547	0.9476	195,887	185,638	13,620	19,091	6,426	11,115
Educational	5,982	0.9148	53,710	49,135	4,351	6,568	1,649	4,044
Flashcards	7,740	1.0966	20,858	22,874	6,382	5,133	4,234	3,312
Total	26,269	0.9526	270,455	257,647	21,710	28,024	10,954	16,875

Table 1: Details of the parallel corpora for spa–shp per domain and in total: $\mathcal{S}$ = number of sentences; $\overline{r}_{\text{shp–spa}}$ = average of the ratio$_{\text{shp–spa}}$ per sentence; $\mathcal{T}$ = number of tokens; $|\mathcal{V}|$ = vocabulary size; HLT = tokens with frequency equals to one.

2 Related work

In Peru, the Quechuan language family has been the primary target in MT. According to the survey of Mager et al. (2018), there are studies in rule-based MT (RBMT), based on the Apertium platform (Forcada et al., 2011), for Quechua Eastern Apurimac (qve) and Quechua Cuzco (quz) (Cavero and Madariaga, 2007). Another study in RBMT, from the project AVENUE, also targeted quz (Monson et al., 2006). Regarding topics closer to SMT, Ortega and Pillaipakkamnatt (2018) improved alignments for a Quechua variant by using an agglutinative language as Finnish as a pivot. The source for their parallel corpus is Rios et al. (2012), so we know that they worked with Quechua Cuzco (quz) too.

Apart from the Quechuan languages, just Aymara in RBMT (Coler and Homola, 2014), and Shipibo-Konibo in SMT (Galarreta et al., 2017) has been studied in MT, with Spanish as their paired language. Besides, the latter is the only Amazonian language in this scope. Moreover, to the best of our knowledge, there are not experiments with neural architectures or further learning strategies for languages of Peru or the Amazon.

Furthermore, and besides the Peruvian scope, there is a large body of knowledge on transfer learning for low-resource MT (Zoph et al., 2016), active learning for MT (Haffari et al., 2009), and collaborative translation (Jiménez-Crespo, 2017).

3 Language specifics

Shipibo-Konibo (shp) belongs to the Panoan language family, and there are more than 30,000 native speakers. It is a morphologically-rich language with agglutinative processes. Besides, there is a preponderance of suffixes in contrast to prefixes, and it includes some clitics particles. In contrast to Spanish, Shipibo-Konibo presents different word orders (e.g. predominance of SOV against SVO), which implies a more challenging scenario.

One of the reasons to target Shipibo-Konibo is the robust capabilities of the ethnic group to preserve its culture and language despite the several years of contact with Spanish speakers (Crevels, 2012). Moreover, they are one of the few native communities in Peru with a socio-political and cultural organisation[1].

Regarding the research and development in language technologies, there are outcomes in different levels, such as a spell-checker (Alva and Oncevay, 2017), a morphological analyser (Cardenas and Zeman, 2018), a lemmatiser with POS-tagger (Pereira-Noriega et al., 2017), a syntax dependency parser (Vásquez et al., 2018) and an SMT system paired with Spanish (Galarreta et al., 2017). Each study includes resources carefully crafted by bilingual speakers and linguists.

4 Dataset

A previous study of spa–shp introduced two corpora: religious and educational (Galarreta et al., 2017). The former is a compilation with post-processing steps of the Bible entries, whereas the latter contains translated sentences of bilingual educational texts from the Peruvian Government[2].

Besides those domains, we introduce a new parallel corpus that was built from a sample of sentences of the Tatoeba project, specifically, the Tab-delimited Bilingual Sentence Pairs in English–Spanish[3]. A few thousands of short sentences were translated from Spanish into Shipibo-Konibo for a certified bilingual translator. We named the new corpus Flashcards, as it is based on flashcards with bilingual sentences to easier memorisation in a language learning context[4].

Table 1 describes the corpus per domain and overall, including information about the number of

---

[1]*Coshikok*: http://www.coshikoxperu.org/
[2]We used an updated version: http://chana.inf.pucp.edu.pe/resources/parallel-corpus/
[3]http://www.manythings.org/anki/
[4]The new parallel corpus is going to be published

translated sentences, an average of the ratio of tokens per sentence between the Shipibo-Konibo and Spanish translations (Galarreta et al., 2017), the total number of tokens, the vocabulary size, and the amount of *hapax legomenon* tokens (HLT) or terms with frequency equals to one.

We observe that the Flashcards domain is proportionally bigger in vocabulary size and HLT regarding the other two, even when the amount of tokens per sentence in average is lower ($\mathcal{T}/\mathcal{S}$). Moreover, the averaged ratio of tokens ($\overline{r}_{\text{shp–spa}}$) has a particular value, as it is the only domain with more tokens per parallel sentence in the Shipibo-Konibo side than in the Spanish one. The following example illustrates a related case:

shp: *Westiora kafe keniresa ea ike.*

spa: *Sólo quería un café.*

eng: *I just wanted a coffee.*

where there is a null subject in Spanish (*ea* or *I*), and Shipibo-Konibo merges *sólo quería* (*just wanted*) into *keniresa* and adds *ike* as an auxiliar.

5 Neural Machine Translation for Shipibo-Konibo

The NMT paradigm has achieved state-of-the-art results mostly with large-resource settings. The training of NMT systems is an open challenge for low-resource language-pairs (Koehn and Knowles, 2017), but we consider a must the alignment to this paradigm, as it is going to be the main focus of the MT research for the following years.

NMT is based on an encoder-decoder framework to perform an end-to-end translation using sequence-to-sequence neural networks (Sutskever et al., 2014). For the encoder, we have a recurrent neural network that receives a source sentence and outputs a dense encoded vector. Similarly, the decoder is another recurrent network that transforms the vector into a target sentence.

In this paper, we use a two-layer encoder-decoder LSTM network. Additionally, we use teacher forcing with 0.5 in the encoder and an attention mechanism in the decoder to look back at the source (Luong et al., 2015). Besides, the number of units of the hidden layer is 1024, the embedding size is 128, and the batch size is 64. We use Adam optimiser and train for ten epochs.

Given the baseline settings, we performed the first experiments at word- and subword-level. For the latter, we use Byte Pair Encoding (BPE) (Sennrich et al., 2016) with different merge operations.

	BLEU_{w}	BLEU_{BPE}	
		5k	15k
Religious	1.29	**2.08**	1.33
Educational	4.10	**4.91**	3.21
Flashcards	**11.95**	11.15	11.11
Total	3.76	**3.94**	2.46

Table 2: BLEU scores with the NMT baseline settings at word- (w) and subword-level using joint BPE with 5,000 (5k) and 15,000 (15k) merge operations for the latter.

Whereas for evaluation, we take 10% of the corpus as development and other 10% as testing sets per each domain and overall.

As we can see in Table 2, the initial results were meagre as expected, with an exception in the new Flashcards domain, where the BLEU score might be higher due to the short length of the sentences. Regarding the subword evaluation with BPE, there are slightly better values in some cases (with the lower amount of merge operations), which is an anticipated trend for the agglomerative nature of the language. Nevertheless, the scores in both religious and educational domains are lower than the SMT system of Galarreta et al. (2017), and the overall result confirms the neediness of using additional strategies for improving the low-resource NMT setting. We examine the next steps only at word-level to control the variables.

5.1 Transfer learning

Following the study of Zoph et al. (2016), we defined a parent language-pair (Spanish to L or spa–L) to benefit a child language-pair (Spanish to Shipibo-Konibo) by pre-initializing parameters of the child using the updated values at the end of the parent training in the encoder-decoder. For exploration purposes, we use a short but diverse set of L languages regarding their potential closeness to Shipibo-Konibo in typological properties.

Table 3 presents the set of languages analysed[5]. The parallel corpora aligned with Spanish is retrieved from several sources: Turkish from OPUS (Tiedemann, 2012), German and Hebrew from the TED Multilingual Parallel Corpus[6], and English from the same source as the new Flashcards corpus. In the case of Hebrew, we transliterated the corpus to the Latin alphabet.

---

[5] We choose four languages to make the experiments: English, German, Turkish and Hebrew. The four languages were chosen due to the availability of the datasets

[6] `https://github.com/ajinkyakulkarni14/`
`TED-Multilingual-Parallel-Corpus`

L (lang.)	$\mathcal{S}_{\text{spa}-L}$	$\text{BLEU}_{\text{spa}-\text{shp}}$	$D_{(\text{shp},L)}$
English	120,566	6.34	0.2822
German	452,661	4.45	0.3382
Turkish	7,177	9.22	**0.1764**
Hebrew	486,466	**12.34**	0.4264

Table 3: Transfer learning experiments using spa–L as a parent language-pair. $\mathcal{S}$ indicates the size of the corpus, BLEU the score of translation in the child language-pair spa–shp, and D is the Hamming distance between L and shp.

	Initial	+ Rand	+ AL
Religious	4.12	4.70	**5.78**
Educational	5.65	5.89	**6.30**
Flashcards	10.20	12.30	**14.71**
Total	9.12	9.75	**10.43**

Table 4: BLEU scores for the 40% incremental step over the initial 50% in the Active Learning experimental setting.

Additionally, we include the transfer learning results for translation, in terms of BLEU score, using the entire spa–shp corpus[7]. We observe that English and German slightly overcome the NMT baseline results; however, Turkish and Hebrew show a significant improvement. The case of Turkish is even more promising, as its corpus size is the smallest among the four languages.

We also present a language similarity score with Shipibo-Konibo. Alike Agić (2017), we compute a language distance using the Hamming distance function with language vectors extracted from the WALS (World Atlas Language Structure) knowledge base of linguistic typology (Dryer and Haspelmath, 2013). We only considered syntactic properties (e.g. word order), as we were performing translation at word-level, and we took advantage of the 103 binary features processed in `lang2vec` (Littell et al., 2017). However, it is worth noting that there are several missing values, specially for Shipibo-Konibo, due to the sparsity of WALS. Thus, we solely preserved the categories with completed entries across the five languages involved, lowering the dimensionality to 68.

A recent study in transfer learning for MT (Kocmi and Bojar, 2018) argued that it might be more important the size of the corpus of the parent language-pair rather than the similarity of the languages concerned. Our results are partially aligned with their claim, but we observe that English and German cannot overcome Turkish despite the large difference in corpus size. However, we cannot derive further conclusions about language distance as a proper measurement for improving transfer learning results, as Hebrew was the most different language, in terms of syntax, and obtained the best translation score in the transfer setup. Nevertheless, we think the metric should be reviewed

carefully, as there are several missing records in WALS. Moreover, the Spanish–Turkish parallel corpus is composed only by GNOME and Ubuntu localisation files, a scanty and limited domain for translation.

A more objective analysis could be performed using similar size and domain corpora, although those requisites are tough to satisfy in MT. Furthermore, if we want to evaluate a subword-level transfer context, we should include morphological features to the language similarity measure as well. Nonetheless, for the next experimental setting, we take as a basis the parameter values learned in the Spanish–Hebrew language-pair.

5.2 Active learning

In this part of the study, we emulate a pool-based active learning setting, where we need to select iterations of sample batches to incrementally improve the MT system. For the sampling query, we partially adapt elemental heuristics proposed for SMT (Haffari et al., 2009). Specifically, we focus on n-gram heuristics (1-gram) to select new sentences based on out-of-vocabulary (OOV) words and term frequency. Due to the high presence of unique and HLT in the corpora, it is relevant to deal with OOV terms, and even more when the target language is an agglutinative one. Besides, this heuristic could be insightful for further subword-level experimentations using BPE.

The evaluation of the active learning approach is performed per domain and altogether. We separate 20% of the parallel corpora as the validation and test sub-sets with 10% each, and the rest of the corpus is used for the pool-based evaluation. We take half of the sentences available as the baseline subset (Initial), and we perform a one-step increment (+40%).

Table 4 presents the BLEU scores, and we observe that the Active Learning criterion achieved better results than random in all the experiments. Although, it is worth noting that the overall results are very low, mainly due to the amount of data

---

[7]We decided not to divide the corpus per domain due to the amount of data, and because we only need the parent language-pair parameters to pre-initialize the next experiment in Active Learning

available. We expect to integrate novel queries and active learning settings proposed directly in the NMT paradigm (Liu et al., 2018). Nevertheless, as the primary goal of the study is the development of a continuous improvement framework, we consider that different AL strategies could offer a proper foundation to incrementally enhance the MT systems for Shipibo-Konibo.

6 Conversational agent prototype for crowd-sourcing

We take inspiration on the actions taken in an humanitarian emergency (Munro, 2010), where there was a need to solve translation queries on-the-fly. In our context, we consider that the endangerment of a native language is an emergency for the community as well, and we would like to reach the speakers to involved them in this revitalisation effort from a computational perspective. Thus, to support the continuous improvement of the MT system developed so far, we expect to retrieve collaborative and crowd-sourced translations from native speakers through social media, which provides extended channels with few access constraints or limitations. For this reason, we decided to build a conversational agent, and we describe our work in progress of the current prototype.

6.1 Interaction strategies

To apply the collaborative learning for translation, we designed a persistent model to support the interaction between the user and the application. The model includes features such as: the storage of potential translations from users and non-translated sentences (in Spanish), the selection of non-translated sentences to be presented to the users, and the integration of the new translations in following training iterations.

The model can be adjusted with different parameters, such as a limited sentence length or term frequency for the selection process, or the number of references translations required from different users given a non-translated sentence. The latter is a significant feature in crowd-sourcing settings, as we cannot assume that a professional translator is going to provide all the feedback, thus, we need to take many references from the crowd to reduce potential noise.

Figure 1: First story: a user requests an automatic translation from Spanish into Shipibo-Konibo. User says: "Translate: This is my life", and the conversational agent answers with the translation ("Traducción")

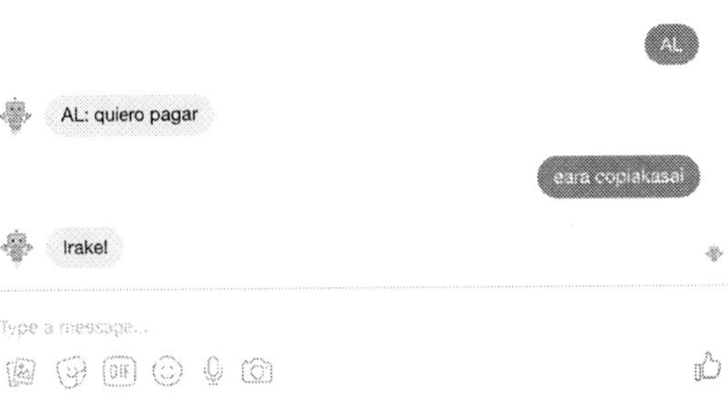

Figure 2: Second story: a user offers its help and the system requests for a new translation. First, the user writes "AL" to start the interaction (more natural expressions are going to be integrated). Then, the system requests for a translation ("I want to pay") and the user answers. Finally, the system ends the interaction with thanks in Shipibo-Konibo.

6.2 Design and implementation

We built a framework for developing a webhook that supports the interaction with the Facebook Messenger API[8] (version 3.2). The webhook supports two types of interactions, known as stories.

The first story refers to requests from users to the conversational agent for translating a phrase or sentence. The translation request must be from Spanish to Shipibo-Konibo, as we can see in Figure 1. The aim of this first story is to engage potential learners interested in the language, or professional translators that want to analyse and post-edit the output of MT systems.

The second story, in contrast with the first one, takes advantage of crowd-sourcing, as it involves a translation requirement from the system to the user after receiving a manifest of support. In Figure 2 we observe the conversational agent asking for the translation of a sentence. The text has been extracted from the pool of non-translated flashcards by using the active learning criterion.

---

[8]We chose this platform because it has been our main communication channel with the certified translators during the corpus development. Official site: `https://developers.facebook.com/docs/graph-api`

6.3 Further development

Apart from technical details to support the model persistence in a large-scale number of interactions, there must be a focus in building a robust communication flow in the stories. For instance, the fist story could be extended to accept feedback of the users in a post-edition setting, although there should be a mechanism to distinguish professional translators from other speakers. In case of the second story, the system could ask to retrieve more translations instead of ending the interaction immediately. Moreover, there should be a usability test for the conversational agent to identify the best interaction flow for the users (native speakers).

7 Conclusion

We presented additional MT results for Shipibo-Konibo using sequence-to-sequence neural networks, altogether with transfer learning and active learning strategies. We also introduced a new parallel corpus domain which texts are used in a language learning context. Overall results are aligned to the amount of data available; however, we observed a promising upward trend in the performance, even more when the new domain is involved. Thus, we integrated an NMT model within a conversational agent prototype to retrieve crowdsourcing and collaborative translations through social media. These have been the initial steps to set up a continuous improvement framework for MT in Shipibo-Konibo.

Furthermore, as we built the current system in the NMT paradigm, we could integrate novel features to steadily improve the performance. Also, we plan to complete the pairwise-system with the translation direction from Shipibo-Konibo into Spanish, and take advantage of monolingual data in Shipibo-Konibo to enhance the encoder-decoder components at subword-level.

Acknowledgments

The authors acknowledge the support of the NVIDIA Corporation with the donation of the Titan Xp GPU used for the study. Moreover, the first author is funded by the "Programa de Apoyo a la Investigación para estudiantes de Posgrado" (Research supporting programme for postgraduate students, PAIP 2018, PUCP), whereas the last author is supported by the EU H2020 GoURMET project under grant agreement No. 825299.

References

Agić, Željko. 2017. Cross-lingual parser selection for low-resource languages. In *Proceedings of the NoDaLiDa 2017 Workshop on Universal Dependencies (UDW 2017)*, pages 1–10.

Alva, Carlo and Arturo Oncevay. 2017. Spell-checking based on syllabification and character-level graphs for a Peruvian agglutinative language. In *Proceedings of the First Workshop on Subword and Character Level Models in NLP*, pages 109–116. Association for Computational Linguistics.

Cardenas, Ronald and Daniel Zeman. 2018. A morphological analyzer for Shipibo-konibo. In *Proceedings of the Fifteenth Workshop on Computational Research in Phonetics, Phonology, and Morphology*, pages 131–139, Brussels, Belgium, October. Association for Computational Linguistics.

Cavero, Indhira Castro and Jaime Farfán Madariaga. 2007. Traductor morfológico del castellano y quechua (Morphological translator of Castilian Spanish and Quechua). *Revista I+ i*, 1(1).

Coler, Matthew and Petr Homola, 2014. *Rule-based machine translation for Aymara*, pages 67–80. Cambridge University Press, 10.

Crevels, Mily, 2012. *Language endangerment in South America: The clock is ticking*, volume 2, pages 176–234. Walter de Gruyter.

Dryer, Matthew S. and Martin Haspelmath, editors. 2013. *WALS Online - World Atlas of Language Structures*. Max Planck Institute for Evolutionary Anthropology, Leipzig.

Forcada, Mikel L, Mireia Ginestí-Rosell, Jacob Nordfalk, Jim ORegan, Sergio Ortiz-Rojas, Juan Antonio Pérez-Ortiz, Felipe Sánchez-Martínez, Gema Ramírez-Sánchez, and Francis M Tyers. 2011. Apertium: a free/open-source platform for rule-based machine translation. *Machine translation*, 25(2):127–144.

Galarreta, Ana Paula, Andrés Melgar, and Arturo Oncevay-Marcos. 2017. Corpus creation and initial SMT experiments between Spanish and Shipibo-konibo. In *Proceedings of the International Conference Recent Advances in Natural Language Processing, RANLP 2017, Varna, Bulgaria, September 2 - 8, 2017*, pages 238–244.

Haffari, Gholamreza, Maxim Roy, and Anoop Sarkar. 2009. Active learning for statistical phrase-based machine translation. In *Proceedings of Human Language Technologies: The 2009 Annual Conference of the North American Chapter of the Association for Computational Linguistics*, pages 415–423, Boulder, Colorado, June. Association for Computational Linguistics.

Jiménez-Crespo, Miguel A. 2017. *Crowdsourcing and online collaborative translations: Expanding the limits of translation studies*, volume 131. John Benjamins Publishing Company.

Kocmi, Tom and Ondřej Bojar. 2018. Trivial transfer learning for low-resource neural machine translation. In *Proceedings of the Third Conference on Machine Translation: Research Papers*, pages 244–252, Belgium, Brussels, October. Association for Computational Linguistics.

Koehn, Philipp and Rebecca Knowles. 2017. Six challenges for neural machine translation. In *Proceedings of the First Workshop on Neural Machine Translation*, pages 28–39. Association for Computational Linguistics.

Littell, Patrick, David R Mortensen, Ke Lin, Katherine Kairis, Carlisle Turner, and Lori Levin. 2017. Uriel and lang2vec: Representing languages as typological, geographical, and phylogenetic vectors. In *Proceedings of the 15th Conference of the European Chapter of the Association for Computational Linguistics: Volume 2, Short Papers*, volume 2, pages 8–14.

Liu, Ming, Wray Buntine, and Gholamreza Haffari. 2018. Learning to actively learn neural machine translation. In *Proceedings of the 22nd Conference on Computational Natural Language Learning*, pages 334–344, Brussels, Belgium, October. Association for Computational Linguistics.

Luong, Minh-Thang, Hieu Pham, and Christopher D Manning. 2015. Effective approaches to attention-based neural machine translation. *arXiv preprint arXiv:1508.04025*.

Mager, Manuel, Ximena Gutierrez-Vasques, Gerardo Sierra, and Ivan Meza-Ruiz. 2018. Challenges of language technologies for the indigenous languages of the Americas. In *Proceedings of the 27th International Conference on Computational Linguistics*, pages 55–69. Association for Computational Linguistics.

Monson, Christian, Ariadna Font Llitjós, Roberto Aranovich, Lori Levin, Ralf Brown, Eric Peterson, Jaime Carbonell, and Alon Lavie. 2006. Building NLP systems for two resource-scarce indigenous languages: Mapudungun and Quechua. *Strategies for developing machine translation for minority languages*, page 15.

Munro, Robert. 2010. Crowdsourced translation for emergency response in Haiti: the global collaboration of local knowledge. In *AMTA 2010 Workshop on Collaborative Crowdsourcing for Translation*, pages 1–4.

Ortega, John and Krishnan Pillaipakkamnatt. 2018. Using morphemes from agglutinative languages like Quechua and Finnish to aid in low-resource translation. In *Proceedings of the AMTA 2018 Workshop on Technologies for MT of Low Resource Languages (LoResMT 2018)*, pages 1–11.

Pereira-Noriega, José, Rodolfo Mercado, Andrés Melgar, Marco Sobrevilla-Cabezudo, and Arturo Oncevay Marcos. 2017. Ship-LemmaTagger: Building an NLP toolkit for a Peruvian native language. In *International Conference on Text, Speech, and Dialogue*, Lecture Notes in Computer Science, pages 473–481. Springer, July.

Rios, Annette, Anne Ghring, and Martin Volk. 2012. Parallel Treebanking Spanish-Quechua: how and how well do they align? *Linguistic Issues in Language Technology*, 7(1).

Sennrich, Rico, Barry Haddow, and Alexandra Birch. 2016. Neural machine translation of rare words with subword units. In *Proceedings of the 54th Annual Meeting of the Association for Computational Linguistics (Volume 1: Long Papers)*, pages 1715–1725, Berlin, Germany, August. Association for Computational Linguistics.

Simons, Gary F. and Charles D. Fenning, editors. 2019. *Ethnologue: Languages of the World. Twenty-second edition*. Dallas Texas: SIL international. Online version: http://www.ethnologue.com.

Sutskever, Ilya, Oriol Vinyals, and Quoc V Le. 2014. Sequence to sequence learning with neural networks. In *Advances in neural information processing systems*, pages 3104–3112.

Tiedemann, Jörg. 2012. Parallel data, tools and interfaces in OPUS. In Calzolari, Nicoletta, Khalid Choukri, Thierry Declerck, Mehmet Uur Doan, Bente Maegaard, Joseph Mariani, Asuncion Moreno, Jan Odijk, and Stelios Piperidis, editors, *Proceedings of the Eight International Conference on Language Resources and Evaluation (LREC'12)*, Istanbul, Turkey, May. European Language Resources Association (ELRA).

Vásquez, Alonso, Renzo Ego Aguirre, Candy Angulo, John Miller, Claudia Villanueva, Željko Agić, Roberto Zariquiey, and Arturo Oncevay. 2018. Toward universal dependencies for Shipibo-konibo. In *Proceedings of the Second Workshop on Universal Dependencies (UDW 2018)*, pages 151–161, Brussels, Belgium, November. Association for Computational Linguistics.

Zoph, Barret, Deniz Yuret, Jonathan May, and Kevin Knight. 2016. Transfer learning for low-resource neural machine translation. In *Proceedings of the 2016 Conference on Empirical Methods in Natural Language Processing*, pages 1568–1575, Austin, Texas, November. Association for Computational Linguistics.

Machine Translation for Crimean Tatar to Turkish

Memduh Gökırmak
ÚFAL
Charles University
Prague, Czechia
memduhg@gmail.com

Francis Morton Tyers
Department of Linguistics
Indiana University
Bloomington, IN, USA
ftyers@iu.edu

Jonathan North Washington
Linguistics Department
Swarthmore College
Swarthmore, PA, USA
jonathan.washington@swarthmore.edu

Abstract

In this paper a machine translation system for Crimean Tatar to Turkish is presented. To our knowledge this is the first Machine Translation system made available for public use for Crimean Tatar, and the first such system released as free and open source software. The system was built using Apertium[1], a free and open source machine translation system, and is currently unidirectional from Crimean Tatar to Turkish. We describe our translation system, evaluate it on parallel corpora and compare its performance with a Neural Machine Translation system, trained on the limited amount of corpora available.

1 Introduction

This paper presents a Free/Open-Source prototype shallow-transfer rule-based machine translation system between Crimean Tatar and Turkish. The system is built using Apertium (Forcada et al., 2010), a free and open source platform that facilitates development of rule-based machine translation systems by providing tools that minimize the

The paper will be laid out as follows: Section 2 gives a short review of some previous work in the area of Turkic–Turkic language machine translation; Section 3 introduces Crimean Tatar and Turkish and compares their grammar; Section 4 describes the system and the tools used to construct it; Section 5 gives an evaluation of the system and compares it with a basic neural translation system,

also presenting an example of a Crimean Tatar sentence and its translations into Turkish by the systems compared.. Finally Section 6 describes our aims for future work and some concluding remarks.

2 Previous work

Within the Apertium project, work on several MT systems between Turkic languages has been started (Turkish–Kyrgyz, Azeri–Turkish, Tatar–Bashkir), but until the release of the pair which this paper presents, the Kazakh–Tatar system (Salimzyanov et al., 2013) was the only one of release level quality, and accordingly the only one released.

Besides these systems and those that are corporately available,[2] a handful of previous works on machine translation systems between Turkic languages exist. MT systems have been reported that translate between Turkish and other Turkic languages, including Turkish–Crimean Tatar (Altıntaş, 2001), Turkish–Azerbaijani (Hamzaoglu, 1993), Turkish–Tatar (Gilmullin, 2008), and Turkish–Turkmen (Tantuğ et al., 2007), though none of these have been released to a public audience. In the development of this system, we use another system developed within the Apertium project, a morphological analyzer for Crimean Tatar (Tyers et al., 2019).

3 Languages

While Turkish and Crimean Tatar belong to different branches of the Turkic family—Oghuz (Southwestern Turkic) and Kypchak (Northwestern Turkic) respectively—historical contact has been intense enough to make the written standards of the two languages somewhat mutually intelligible, although differences in modern vocabulary prevent more complete mutual intelligibility.

[1] http://wiki.apertium.org

[2] e.g., Google Translate, http://translate.google.com

Turkish is the official language in Turkey, and an official language in Cyprus. It is a recognized minority language in Greece, Iraq, Kosovo, Macedonia and Romania. There are around 80 million fluent speakers of Turksih, mostly living in Turkey (Eberhard et al., 2019). Crimean Tatar is a recognized minority language in Ukraine and Romania. There are over half a million speakers of Crimean Tatar, who mostly live in the Crimean peninsula, Uzbekistan, Turkey, Romania, and Bulgaria (Eberhard et al., 2019). The map in Figure 1 shows the two languages' situation among other Turkic languages spoken around the Black Sea.

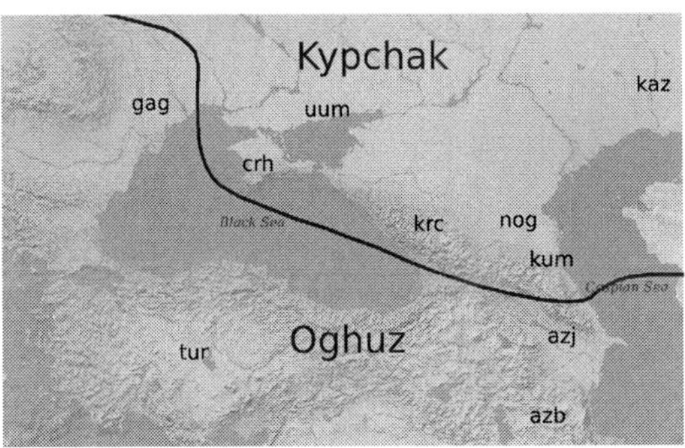

Figure 1: Location of Turkish (`tur`) and Crimean Tatar (`crh`) within the Black Sea area.

Turkish has undergone a purification process, removing many Arabic and Persian-origin words that it had in common with Crimean Tatar. Turkish has been influenced by and borrowed words mainly from French throughout the 20th century, while the major influence on Crimean Tatar has been Russian. Consider for example the loan word for "bus station", Turkish *otogar* < Fra. "auto- + gare" and Crimean Tatar *avtovokzal* < Rus. "автовокзал".

3.1 Orthographic and Phonological differences

Both the orthographies and the phonologies of the languages are remarkably close, especially in the written standard, but a number of differences are immediately observable at first glance.

The most obvious phonological differences between Crimean Tatar and Turkish are the existence of three phonemes in Crimean Tatar that do not exist in Turkish: /q/, /ʁ/, and /ŋ/.

There are also differences in the treatment of loanwords. Word-final stops at the end of recent loandwords are more consistently devoiced in Turkish, as can be seen in Turkish *mikrop* 'microbe' and Crimean Tatar *mikrob*, or *sülfit* 'sulphide' and *sul-*

fid. The affricate /ts/ is usually realised as /s/ in Turkish, but preserved in Crimean Tatar. For example, words like Crimean Tatar *tsilindir* 'cylinder', *tsellofan* 'cellophane' tend to appear as *silindir* and *selofan* in Turkish. However, examples such as tsunami do appear in Turkish, and it may also be important that Turkish loans of this sort tend to be of French or English origin, while the Crimean Tatar loanwords are usually from Russian.

3.1.1 Latin script

In recent years, Crimean Tatar has for the most part employed a latin script almost identical to the Turkish script with the exception of a few letters. The letter *q* is used to represent /q/, a voiceless uvular stop in Crimean Tatar. Neither the sound nor the letter exists in standard Turkish. Crimean Tatar also tends to mark long *a* sounds /a:/ more consistently with a circumflex, *â*, than Turkish, where the character is used sporadically and for more ambiguous purposes — i.e. it can also be used to mark palatalisation. The letter *ñ*, also not used in Turkish, is used for the dorsal nasal /ŋ/, which for the most part no longer exists in Turkish. The use of the letter *ğ* also differs. In Turkish, *ğ* represents what was once a dorsal obstruent, but has since deleted in modern standard Turkish and caused compensatory lengthening of a preceding vowel, e.g. *dağı* [dɑː.ɯ] 'mountain–POSS.3'. In Crimean Tatar, the letter *ğ* represents a uvular fricative /ʁ/, e.g. *dağı* [dɑʁɯ] 'mountain–POSS.3'.

3.1.2 Cyrillic

A Cyrillic alphabet based on that of Russian was used officially from 1938 to the 1990s, and has still not completely fallen out of use today. Unlike some of the other Turkic alphabets, it did not feature special characters that were not present in the Russian alphabet. Consonants and vowels that did not exist in Russian were instead written using digraphs, often involving the hard ъ or soft ь sign.

For example, the consonants represented as *q*, *ğ* and *ñ* in the Latin script are represented as къ, гъ, and нъ, respectively, in the Cyrillic orthography. Also, the vowels represented with *ü* and *ö* in the Latin script are represented with either уь and оь, or *y* and *o* with a ь after the following consonant, or just *y* and *o* in the presence of certain consonants. See (Tyers et al., 2019) for more details, and how the transliteration module is used to process Cyrillic Crimean Tatar input.

The sentence "Welcome to Crimea!" is shown in

lang. / orthography	text
Crim. Tatar Latin	Qırımǧa hoş keldiñiz!
Crim. Tatar Cyrillic	Къырымгъа хош кельдинъиз!
Crim. Tatar IPA	[qɯɾɯmʁa xoʃ keldiŋiz]
Turkish	Kırım'a hoş geldiniz!
Turkish IPA	[kɯɾɯma hoʃ gʲɛldiniz]

Table 1: "Welcome to Crimea" in Latin and Cyrillic Crimean Tatar orthographies with a Turkish translation.

the Latin and Cyrillic orthographies along with the Turkish translation in Table 1.

3.2 Morphological Differences

The morpheme *-A*, which marks the aorist in Crimean Tatar, serves as the optative mood in Turkish. And while the Turkish aorist *-Ir/-Ar* exists in Crimean Tatar, it is used as a future tense.

Both languages have two basic morphemes for the past tense: Turkish *-mIş* and *-DI* and Crimean Tatar *-GAn*[3] and *-DI*. In Turkish, the distinction is between non-first-hand evidential past and first-hand evidential past, whereas in Crimean Tatar the distinction is between non-recent past and recent past. In Crimean Tatar, evidential tenses are usually formed with the additional morpheme *eken*.

Furthermore, Crimean Tatar does not have a distinct strategy for marking progressive aspect, and uses the same morpheme for both non-past and present progressive. In Turkish, the progressive is marked by *-(I)yor*, and can be used with a variety of tenses. Both languages, however, have a progressive construct used in more formal speech and writing, *-mAktA*, which comprises a gerund in locative case.

A number of phonological differences exist between cognate inflectional morphemes in the two lanuages: for example, the Crimean Tatar dative case *-GA*, which can be realised as *-ǧa, -ge, -qa, -ke* depending on its phonological environment, corresponds to *-(y)A* in Turkish, realised as *-a, -e, -ya, ye* depending on phonological environment.

3.3 Syntactic differences

Turkish has a richer inventory of morphology relating to relative clauses, particularly verbal adverbs. However, Crimean Tatar exhibits more auxiliary verbs, which are used to add modal and aspectual information to verb phrases.

The languages also differ in their placement of the polar question particle *-mI* relative to person agreement suffixes: in Crimean Tatar the question particle comes after person agreement, whereas in Turkish it tends to come before. For example, in Crimean Tatar *bilesiñmi* 'do you know?' the question particle follows the 2nd person singular agreement suffix *-sIñ*, whereas in the corresponding Turkish form *biliyor musun*, the question particle preceds the agreement suffix *-sIn*.

4 System

The system is based on the Apertium machine translation platform (Forcada et al., 2010).[4] While initially developed to translated between closely related Romance languages such as Catalan and Spanish, the system has evolved to handle different and more distantly related languages. Apertium's code and data are licensed under the Free Software Foundation's General Public Licence[5] (GPL) and all the software and data for the 47 currently released languages (and other pairs being worked on) is available for download from GitHub.[6]

4.1 Architecture of the system

The Apertium translation engine consists of a Unix-style pipeline or assembly line with the following modules (see Figure 2):

- A deformatter which encapsulates format information from the input in superblanks which the other modules process as blanks between words.

- A morphological analyser, implemented as a transducer, which processes surface forms (SF) (words, or, where detected, multiword lexical units or MWLUs) and produces one or more lexical forms (LF) consisting of lemma, part of speech and morphological information.

- A module that disambiguates between possible analyses depending on the context.

- A lexical transfer module which reads each source-language (SL) LF and produces corresponding target-language (TL) LFs by looking them up in a bilingual dictionary encoded as an FST compiled from the corresponding XML

---

[3]The Crimean Tatar morpheme *-GAn* is cognate to the Turkish participle form *-(y)An*.

[4]http://www.apertium.org
[5]https://www.gnu.org/licenses/gpl.html
[6]https://github.com/apertium

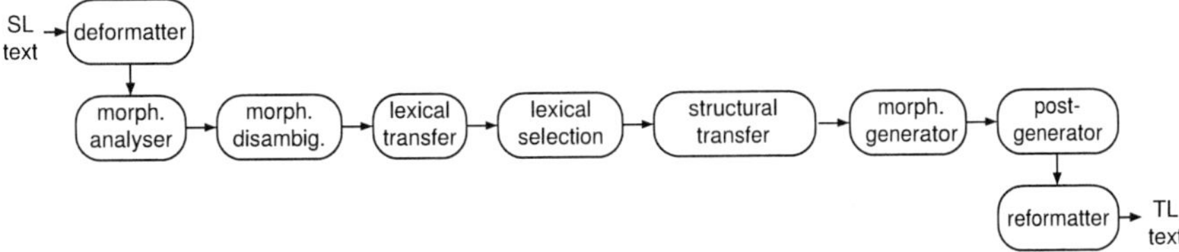

Figure 2: System Architecture

file. The lexical transfer module may return more than one TL LF for a single SL LF.

- A lexical selection module which uses rules to choose the best translation of ambiguous source language LFs based on context.

- Transfer rules that work with a shallow method to change grammatical structures in the source language to ones more befitting the target language.

- A morphological generator that produces a TL SF for each TL LF, by applying the correct inflection.

- A post-generator FST to deal with minor orthographic issues.

- A reformatter which de-encapsulates any format information.

The modules are discussed in the following sections.

4.2 Morphological transducers

The morphological transducers are based on the popular Helsinki Finite State Technology (Linden et al., 2011), a free/open-source reimplementation of the Xerox finite-state toolchain. It provides both the lexc formalism for defining lexicons and the twol and xfst formalisms for modelling morphophonological rules. Along with its open-source license, this toolkit is used as it — or the equivalent XFST — has been widely used for other Turkic languages (Cöltekin, 2010; Altıntaş and Çiçekli, 2001; Tantuğ et al., 2006; Washington et al., 2012; Tyers et al., 2012b).

The morphologies of both languages are implemented in lexc, and the morphophonologies of both languages are implemented in twol. Use of lexc allows for straightforward definition of different word classes and subclasses. For example, Crimean Tatar

and Turkish have two classes of verbs that have different vowels in the aorist morpheme. Class membership cannot be predicted based on any phonological criteria and is simply a lexical property of any given verb. For example, the Turkish verbs *ısır* and *kır*, "bite" and "break" respectively, inflect differently in the aorist, as *ısırır* and *kırar*. Despite the otherwise identical rules of vowel harmony, these two verbs require different paradigms for inflection. This was implemented in lexc with two similar sets of continuation lexica that lead to the appropriate affixes for a given word class.

Twol allows for simple implementation of phonological phenomena such as vowel harmony or voicing/devoicing.

4.3 Bilingual lexicon

The bilingual lexicon currently contains 9,269 stem-to-stem correspondences and was built by:

- Crossing a Crimean-Tatar to Russian + Russian to Turkish dictionary

- Searching for cognates using regular expressions to change frequent differences, e.g. Turkish *hava*, "air", vs. Crimean Tatar *ava*, or similarly *hoca*, "teacher", vs. *oca*

- Consulting a Crimean Tatar to Russian Dictionary manually[7]

- Consulting a Turkish (Ottoman) dictionary[8]

- Adding words provided by Kemal Altıntaş, used in his work on Turkish to Crimean Tatar machine translation (Altıntaş, 2001).

Entries are mostly one-to-one stem correspondences given with their parts of speech, but some also have ambiguous translations.

---

[7] `http://medeniye.org/lugat`
[8] `http://lugatim.org`

4.4 Disambiguation rules

We use Constraint Grammar (CG) (Karlsson et al., 1995) for contextual rule-based disambiguation between the possible analyses the analyzer produces for each surface form. The version of the formalism used is vislcg3.[9] The analyzer outputs are fairly ambiguous with an average of around 2.13 analyses per form for Crimean Tatar and 2.09 for Turkish. Using the disambiguator, ambiguity is currently down to 1.18 analyses per form for Crimean Tatar and 1.46 for Turkish.

The level of ambiguity has still not converged to near 1, due to many ambiguous affixes that both languages have, particularly in non-finite verbal morphology. However the downside to this is minimized by the fact that the closely related grammar of the two languages means that the very same ambiguity can often carry over in translation without causing an error.

4.5 Lexical selection rules

We use the Apertium lexical selection module (Tyers et al., 2012a).

In some instances, even word translations that are direct cognates may be used in different contexts in the source and target languages. For example, Crimean Tatar *vaqıt* is a word expressing a temporal concept, either a certain point in time or a duration. Turkish has a cognate with very similar meanings, *vakit*, but different contexts elicit different interpretations. Certain collocations such as *bir vaqıt*, "(for) some time", require the use of another translation in Turkish, *süre*. A lexical selection rule to choose the translation *süre* when it occurs with *bir* is written to make sure the correct translation is produced. Similarly the Crimean Tatar word *zümre* has a direct cognate in Turkish, however when it is used in the sense of a language family, it must be translated into Turkish as *aile*, literally "family." The system currently has a total of 13 lexical selection rules.

4.6 Structural transfer rules

Structural transfer rules are written in XML files and are applied left-to-right and longest match first. With equal length matches the preceding rule in the file prevails. There are currently 53 rules for translation from Crimean Tatar to Turkish, and 9 for Turkish to Crimean Tatar.

crh Sentence	Kerekmey maña öyle feodallar.
Ref. Translation	Lazım değil bana öyle feodaller.
RBMT Output	Gerekmez bana öyle feodallar.
NMT Output	Gerekmez bana **böyle otlaklar**.

Table 2: Example of MT output for a `crh` input sentence.

5 Evaluation

All evaluation was tested against version 0.2.1, or r53f133c in the Apertium GitHub.

5.1 Coverage

Lexical coverage of the system is calculated over freely available corpora of Crimean Tatar. Two years worth of content (2014 and 2015) from Radio Free Europe / Radio Liberty (RFERL)'s Crimean Tatar service,[10] as well as a recent dump of Wikipedia's articles in Crimean Tatar were used.

Corpus	Coverage	Wordcount
Krymr2014	92.6%	874,662
Krymr2015	93.7%	798,666
Wikipedia	89.7%	198,178
Total	**92.8**	**2,032,300**

Table 3: Coverage over corpora. We define coverage here as the percentage of words in the corpus that the system analyzes and produces a translation for.

As shown in Table 3, the naïve coverage of the Crimean Tatar-Turkish MT system over the news corpora approaches that of a broad-coverage MT system, and has less than a tenth of words unknown. The coverage over the Wikipedia corpus is slightly worse, due to the fact that this corpus is "dirtier": it contains orthographical errors, wiki code, repetitions, as well as quite a few proper nouns.

5.2 Translation Quality

Table 2 shows a Crimean Tatar sentence and its translations by both our RBMT system and the NMT system. In both the sentence "I don't need feudal types like that," is translated with *gerekmez* instead of the equivalent *lazım değil*. The RBMT preserves the meaning but doesn't produce the correct vowel harmony in *feodaller*, and the NMT produces the translation "I don't need pastures like this."

---

[9] `http://visl.sdu.dk/cg3.html`
[10] `https://ktat.krymr.com/`

We use the metrics BLEU (Papineni et al., 2002) and Word Error Rate, a metric based on Levenshtein distance (Levenshtein, 1966) to evaluate our system on parallel corpora and compare it with the performance of a Neural Machine Translation system trained on the same corpora. We use an *NMT-Small* model from the OpenNMT (Klein et al., 2017) framework for the neural translation. The model we train is word-level, using Byte-pair Encoding (Sennrich et al., 2015).

To evaluate our system the need arises for parallel corpora. While aligned sentences ready for MT training are not available, a number of academic works published in Turkey provide Crimean Tatar–language text along with Turkish translations. These works are mostly collections of folk tales (Bakırcı, 2010) and selections from Crimean Tatar literature in the Soviet period, from sources including the literary journal *Yıldız* (Atıcı, 2008; Hendem, 2008) and the works of Ayder Osman (Akın, 2014). Other sources deal with the literature of a certain period (Hakyemez, 2007) or social/political phenomenon (Türkaslan, 2015). We align and tokenize the sentences in these parallel corpora using hunalign (Varga et al., 2007) and the tokenizer script provided with the Moses statistical translation toolkit (Koehn et al., 2007). We are in negotiation with the rights holders to release the gathered corpus under an open licence.

Corpus	crh Tokens	tur Tokens
Yıldız (Volume I)	192,671	190,769
Yıldız (Volume II)	161,047	160,420
Ayder Osman	22,190	21,950
Poverty Literature	23,701	24,185
Folk Tales	84,499	78,998

Table 4: Parallel Corpora. We join together all of these corpora except for the folk tales, and split this in a 90-5-5 split. We use the 5% test portion and the folk tales to test and compare the NMT and

We use all of the parallel corpora listed in Table 4 except for the folk tales in NMT training, randomizing the order of their sentences and splitting them into train, testing and development sets of roughly 90%, 5% and 5% in proportion. This amounts to about 360 thousand tokens for each language in the training corpora, 20 thousand each for the development corpus and again 20 thousand each for testing. The folk tales corpus has a slightly different orthographic system from standard Crimean Tatar, and is

Corpus	System	BLEU	WER
Test Corpus	RBMT	20.50	54.83%
Test Corpus	NMT	7.88	76.25%
Test Corpus	None	8.29	69.49%
Folk Tales	RBMT	22.07	52.63%
Folk Tales	NMT	2.27	85.11%
Folk Tales	None	9.04	67.87%

Table 5: Evaluation of Translation Quality. "None" simply measures the BLEU and WER scores on corresponding untranslated parallel sentences in each language.

non-trivial to convert into the standard. We use this corpus as another test corpus, to compare the performance of our RBMT (Rule-based Machine Translation) and NMT (Neural Machine Translation) systems in situations showing orthographic or dialectal variety.

Table 5 compares the performance of RBMT and NMT on the system, and provides scores for when translation is not done at all in the rows where the System column is filled with "None." The Rule-based system performs better than the Neural system, in both the WER and BLEU metrics. A number of reasons could factor into this. The orthographic and dialectal variety of the texts used in the aligned corpora may have hindered learning and generalization in the NMT system. The RBMT system is to some degree robust to this, as adding frequent variants of frequent words is a simple issue, and one that we frequently addressed while developing the RBMT system on the Wikipedia and news corpora. It should be noted that none of the parallel corpora used for evaluation were used while developing the RBMT system, including the train and development sets.

The majority of RBMT errors are mostly due either to mistakes and gaps in the morphophonology components and disambiguation errors or input words being out of the vocabulary. The NMT errors, however, seem to stem from simple lack of data. The figures achieved given only 360 thousand tokens of training data on each side seems to be consistent with experiments conducted in the literature concerning the relation of NMT performance and the amount of data (Koehn and Knowles, 2017). Taken along with the relative lack of standardization of the language, this should account to some degree for the poor performance.

The sheer similarity (and not inconsiderable mutual intelligibility) of the two languages also benefits the RBMT and the scenario where no system at all is used, in comparison to an NMT system that does not have adequate data to encode and decode input text properly.

6 Conclusion

To our knowledge we have presented the first ever publicly available MT system between Crimean Tatar and Turkish, which is available online for use on Apertium's website.[11] It has near production-level coverage, but is rather prototype-level in terms of the number of rules. Although the impact of this relatively low number of rules on the quality of translation is extensive, the outlook is promising and the current results suggest that a high-quality translation between morphologically-rich agglutinative languages is possible.

We have evaluated our system on an amount of parallel corpora gathered by linguistics departments in Turkey, and compared the performance with that of an NMT system trained on these corpora. The results indicate that even in 2019, it is feasible to use RBMT between closely related, morphologically rich languages when there are not enough resources to train the cutting edge in Neural Machine Translation.

We plan to continue development on the pair; the coverage of the system is already quite high, although we intend to increase it to 95% on the larger monolingual corpora we have — we estimate that this will mean adding around 5,000 new stems and take 1–2 months. The remaining work will be improving the quality of translation by adding more rules, starting with the CG module. The long-term plan is to integrate the data created with other open-source data for Turkic languages in order to make transfer systems between all the Turkic language pairs. Related work is currently ongoing with Kazakh–Turkish, Uyghur–Turkish, Sakha–Kazakh and (Kazan) Tatar–Turkish. The system is available as free/open-source software under the GNU GPL, and the whole system may be downloaded from GitHub.

Acknowledgements

We would like to thank the anonymous reviewers for their insightful comments on the paper and our colleagues Remziye Berberova, Darya Kavitskaya and Nick Howell who contributed to the development of the components of the system specific to Crimean Tatar. The work was done with financial support from Google's Summer of Code program[12], for which we are also grateful.

References

Akın, Serkan. 2014. Review of the stories named "bizim gemimiz", "yıllar ve dostlar", "biz bir dünyada yaşaymız" and "demircinin teklifi" by ayder osman. Master's thesis, Gazi University, Ankara.

Altıntaş, Kemal. 2001. Turkish to Crimean Tatar machine translation system. Master's thesis, Bilkent University.

Altıntaş, Kemal and Ilyas Çiçekli. 2001. A morphological analyser for Crimean Tatar. In *Proceedings of the 10th Turkish Symposium on Artificial Intelligence and Neural Networks (TAINN'2001)*, pages 180–189.

Atıcı, Abdülkadir. 2008. Crimean Tatar Compilations from the Journal Yıldız (Volume I). Master's thesis, Ege University, İzmir.

Bakırcı, Nedim. 2010. *Crimean Tatar Folk Tales*. Kömen Publishing, Konya, Turkey.

Cöltekin, Çağrı. 2010. A freely available morphological analyzer for Turkish. In *LREC*, volume 2, pages 19–28.

Eberhard, David M., Gary F. Simons, and Charles D. Fennig, editors. 2019. *Ethnologue: Languages of the World*. SIL International, Dallas, Texas, twenty-second edition. Online version: http://www.ethnologue.com.

Forcada, Mikel L., Mireia Ginestí Rosell, Jacob Nordfalk, Jim O'Regan, Sergio Ortiz-Rojas, Juan Antonio Pérez-Ortiz, Gema Ramírez-Sánchez, Felipe Sánchez-Martínez, and Francis M. Tyers. 2010. Apertium: a free/open-source platform for rule-based machine translation platform. *Machine Translation*.

Gilmullin, R. A. 2008. The Tatar-Turkish machine translation based on the two-level morphological analyzer. *Interactive Systems and Technologies: The Problems of Human-Computer Interaction*, pages 179–186.

Hakyemez, Betül. 2007. Selected Stories from Crimean Tatar Literature in the period 1928-1937. Master's thesis, Marmara University, Istanbul.

Hamzaoglu, Ilker. 1993. Machine translation from Turkish to other Turkic languages and an implementation for the Azeri language. Master's thesis, Bogazici University, Istanbul.

Hendem, Elif. 2008. Crimean Tatar Compilations from the Journal Yıldız (Volume II). Master's thesis, Ege University, İzmir.

---

[11]https://www.apertium.org/?dir=crh-tur

[12]summerofcode.withgoogle.com

Karlsson, Fred, Atro Voutilainen, Juha Heikkilae, and Arto Anttila. 1995. *Constraint Grammar: a language-independent system for parsing unrestricted text*, volume 4. Walter de Gruyter.

Klein, Guillaume, Yoon Kim, Yuntian Deng, Jean Senellart, and Alexander M Rush. 2017. OpenNMT: Open-source toolkit for neural machine translation. *arXiv preprint arXiv:1701.02810*.

Koehn, Philipp and Rebecca Knowles. 2017. Six challenges for neural machine translation. *arXiv preprint arXiv:1706.03872*.

Koehn, Philipp, Hieu Hoang, Alexandra Birch, Chris Callison-Burch, Marcello Federico, Nicola Bertoldi, Brooke Cowan, Wade Shen, Christine Moran, Richard Zens, et al. 2007. Moses: Open source toolkit for statistical machine translation. In *Proceedings of the 45th annual meeting of the association for computational linguistics companion volume proceedings of the demo and poster sessions*, pages 177–180.

Levenshtein, Vladimir I. 1966. Binary codes capable of correcting deletions, insertions, and reversals. In *Soviet physics doklady*, volume 10, pages 707–710.

Linden, Krister, Miikka Silfverberg, Erik Axelson, Sam Hardwick, and Tommi Pirinen, 2011. *HFST–Framework for Compiling and Applying Morphologies*, volume 100 of *Communications in Computer and Information Science*, pages 67–85.

Papineni, Kishore, Salim Roukos, Todd Ward, and Wei-Jing Zhu. 2002. Bleu: a method for automatic evaluation of machine translation. In *Proceedings of the 40th annual meeting on association for computational linguistics*, pages 311–318. Association for Computational Linguistics.

Salimzyanov, Ilnar, J Washington, and F Tyers. 2013. A free/open-source Kazakh-Tatar machine translation system. *Machine Translation Summit XIV*.

Sennrich, Rico, Barry Haddow, and Alexandra Birch. 2015. Neural machine translation of rare words with subword units. *arXiv preprint arXiv:1508.07909*.

Tantuğ, A Cüneyd, Eşref Adalı, and Kemal Oflazer. 2006. Computer analysis of the Turkmen language morphology. In *Advances in Natural Language Processing*, pages 186–193. Springer.

Tantuğ, A Cüneyd, Eşref Adalı, and Kemal Oflazer. 2007. A mt system from turkmen to turkish employing finite state and statistical methods.

Tyers, Francis M., Felipe Sánchez-Martínez, Mikel L Forcada, et al. 2012a. Flexible finite-state lexical selection for rule-based machine translation.

Tyers, Francis M., Jonathan North Washington, Ilnar Salimzyanov, and Rustam Batalov. 2012b. A prototype machine translation system for Tatar and Bashkir based on free/open-source components. In *First Workshop on Language Resources and Technologies for Turkic Languages*, page 11.

Tyers, Francis M., Jonathan North Washington, Darya Kavitskaya, Memduh Gökırmak, Nick Howell, and Remizye Berberova. 2019. A biscriptual morphological transducer for Crimean Tatar. In *Proceedings of the 3rd Workshop on the Use of Computational Methods in the Study of Endangered Languages*.

Türkaslan, Nesibe. 2015. Poverty Literature in Crimean Tatars [sic]. Master's thesis, Gazi University, Ankara.

Varga, Dániel, Péter Halácsy, András Kornai, Viktor Nagy, László Németh, and Viktor Trón. 2007. Parallel corpora for medium density languages. *Amsterdam Studies In The Theory And History Of Linguistic Science Series 4*, 292:247.

Washington, Jonathan, Mirlan Ipasov, and Francis Tyers. 2012. A finite-state morphological transducer for Kyrgyz. In Chair), Nicoletta Calzolari (Conference, Khalid Choukri, Thierry Declerck, Mehmet Uğur Doğan, Bente Maegaard, Joseph Mariani, Asuncion Moreno, Jan Odijk, and Stelios Piperidis, editors, *Proceedings of the Eighth International Conference on Language Resources and Evaluation (LREC'12)*, Istanbul, Turkey, may. European Language Resources Association (ELRA).

Developing a Neural Machine Translation System for Irish

Arne Defauw, Sara Szoc, Tom Vanallemeersch, Anna Bardadym, Joris Brabers, Frederic Everaert, Kim Scholte, Koen Van Winckel, Joachim Van den Bogaert

CrossLang
Kerkstraat 106
9050 Gentbrugge
Belgium
{firstname.lastname}@crosslang.com

Abstract

In this paper we develop a neural machine translation (NMT) system for translating from English into Irish and vice versa. We evaluate the performance of NMT on the resource-poor English-Irish (EN–GA) language pair, show that we can achieve good translation quality in comparison to previously reported systems, and outperform Google Translate™ with several BLEU points on a domain-specific test set related to the legal domain. We show that back-translation of monolingual data closely related to the domain of the test set can further increase the model's performance. Finally, we present a lightweight method for filtering synthetic sentence pairs obtained via back-translation using a tool for misalignment detection. We show that our approach results in a slightly higher BLEU score while requiring less training data.

1   Introduction

In recent years the performance of machine translation systems has been improving significantly thanks to the shift from statistical machine translation (SMT) to NMT. Replacing the recurrent neural network (RNN) architecture with a Transformer architecture that relies entirely on self-attention to compute representations of its input and output has set a new state of the art in the field of machine translation (Vaswani et al. 2017).

However, for low-resource languages, the performance of (neural) machine translation systems can still be disappointing, as pointed out for instance by Koehn et al. (2017). Many approaches have been suggested to improve the quality of NMT in such a low-resource setting, among which multilingual models (Johnson et al. 2016; Thanh-Le et al. 2016), unsupervised approaches (Lample et al. 2019) and systems relying on back-translation (Sennrich et al. 2016) have been the most successful.

In this paper we focus on the translation of the English-Irish language pair using NMT. The Irish language has been categorized as a 'weak or not supported language' by the META-NET report (Judge et al. 2012) due to the lack of good translation resources. Despite this relatively low availability of resources, both in terms of monolingual and bilingual content, it has been shown that an SMT system can achieve promising translation quality both in a domain-specific setting (Dowling et al. 2015) and in a more broad-domain context (Arcan et al. 2016).

First steps were taken by Dowling et al. (2018) to apply NMT methods to EN–GA MT, although the resulting NMT system performed significantly worse than SMT, scoring more than 6 BLEU lower on an in-domain test set.[1]

In this work we will further explore the potential of NMT for the EN–GA language pair. We add web-crawled parallel data to the publicly available resources used in previous studies and show relatively good translation quality both on a domain-specific test set and on a more generic test set. Next, our experiments confirm that NMT translation quality for GA→EN can be significantly improved using back-translation.

---

[1] Reported BLEU score of 40.1, compared to a BLEU score of 46.4 for the SMT system.

Due to a lack of Irish monolingual data, back-translation was less useful for EN→GA NMT.

Finally, a set of experiments was performed in which the synthetic parallel corpus, obtained via back-translation, was filtered with Bicleaner[2] (Sánchez-Cartagena et al. 2018), a tool for misalignment detection. We show that applying misalignment detection on a synthetic corpus before adding it to the parallel training data results in small increases in BLEU score and could be a useful strategy in terms of data selection.

Filtering of parallel data has been the subject of various studies (Axelrod et al. 2011; van der Wees et al. 2017), but such data selection methods have only been scarcely investigated in the context of back-translation. Fadaee et al. (2018) suggest several sampling strategies for synthetic data obtained via back-translation, targeting difficult to predict words. More closely related to our filtering technique is the method proposed by Imankulova et al. (2017). They present a method in which a synthetic corpus was filtered by calculating the BLEU score between the target monolingual sentence and the translation of the synthetic source sentence in the target language and report small increases in translation quality in a low-resource setting.

2 Materials and methods

2.1 Data

In this section, we give an overview of the data used for training our NMT systems. Both bilingual and monolingual data are used.

In Table 1 an overview of the parallel data is shown. Three types of data were collected: 1) Baseline data, i.e. a collection of publicly available resources; 2) Web-crawled data, i.e. data scraped from two bilingual websites, and 3) ParaCrawl data.

The baseline data has been described in detail in previous publications (Dowling et al. 2015; Arcan et al. 2016). We note that there are some other parallel corpora available for the EN–GA language pair, the largest of which are the *KDE*[3]

and *GNOME*[4] corpora. However, due to the very specific nature of these corpora, they were not included in the training data.

The web-crawled dataset consists of sentence pairs we scraped and aligned ourselves from two bilingual websites. This data was scraped using Scrapy[5] and then document-aligned using Malign,[6] a tool for document alignment that makes use of MT. Sentence alignment of these document pairs was subsequently performed using Hunalign[7] (Varga et al. 2005). Finally, the misalignment detection tool Bicleaner (Sánchez-Cartagena et al. 2018) was applied to these aligned sentences (the Bicleaner threshold was set to 0.5[8]).

Parallel corpus	#unique sentence pairs	#EN tokens
DGT[9]	38,672	948,037
+ DCEP[10]	7,303	158,035
+ EU Bookshop[11]	95,705	2,182,873
+ Irish legislation[12]	172,272	4,285,570
+ EU constitution[13]	6,702	140,101
= **Baseline data**	**315,748**	**7,634,954**
www.education.ie	128,016	3,408,864
+ www.courts.ie	2,791	66,260
= **Web-crawled data**	**130,807**	**3,475,124**
ParaCrawl data[14] (0.5<Bicleaner score)	**784,606**	**17,646,315**
Total	**1,195,067**	**27,860,572**

Table 1 Parallel NMT training data (EN–GA)

We also used the ParaCrawl corpus as a bilingual resource. We used the Raw EN–GA ParaCrawl corpus v4.0[15] consisting of 156M sentence pairs. ParaCrawl is known to contain a diversity of noise such as misalignments, untranslated sentences, non-linguistic characters, wrong encoding, language errors, short segments etc. that may harm NMT performance (Khayrallah et al. 2018). Therefore, only pairs with a Bicleaner score

---

[2] https://github.com/bitextor/bicleaner

[3] http://opus.nlpl.eu/KDE4.php

[4] http://opus.nlpl.eu/GNOME.php

[5] https://scrapy.org

[6] Now part of the ParaCrawl pipeline: https://github.com/bitextor/bitextor

[7] http://mokk.bme.hu/en/resources/hunalign

[8] Threshold based on manual inspection.

[9] http://opus.nlpl.eu/DGT.php

[10] https://wt-public.emm4u.eu/Resources/DCEP-2013/DCEP-Download-Page.html

[11] http://opus.nlpl.eu/EUbookshop-v2.php

[12] http://www.gaois.ie/en

[13] http://opus.nlpl.eu/EUconst.php

[14] https://paracrawl.eu

[15] https://s3.amazonaws.com/web-language-models/paracrawl/release3/en-ga.classify.gz

greater than 0.5 were considered. After deduplication, the size of the ParaCrawl corpus diminishes to 784k sentence pairs.

We extracted two test sets from this parallel data: a domain-specific test set (legal domain) and a more generic test set, both consisting of 3k sentence pairs, and held out from the *Irish Legislation* and *EU Constitution* corpora (legal) and the *DGT* and *DCEP* corpora (generic), respectively. We note that the *DGT* corpus is derived from the translation memories of the European Commission's Directorate-General for Translation, while the *DCEP* corpus originates from the European Parliament. While both are linked to the administrative text type, the *DCEP* corpus includes a wider variety of text types compared to the former (Hajlaoui et al. 2014).

In comparison to previous publications, two relatively large EN–GA corpora could not be used in this work, due to their not being publicly available: 1) a set of translation memory files from the Department of Arts, Heritage and the Gaeltacht (DAHG), containing approximately 40k parallel sentences (Dowling et al. 2015); 2) translations of second level textbooks (Cuimhne na dTéacsleabhar) in the domain of economics and geography, holding around 350k sentence pairs (Arcan et al. 2016).

Monolingual EN corpus	#unique EN sentences	#EN tokens
DCEP	2,004,062	52,163,146
+ DGT	1,644,325	39,468,227
+ EAC[16]	1,341	21,828
+ ECDC[17]	2,027	35,935
+ JRC-Acquis[18]	463,073	13,316,245
= **Total**	**3,989,791**	**102,178,555**
Monolingual GA corpus	#unique GA sentences	#GA tokens
Wikipedia	217,695	6,540,334
+ ParaCrawl corpus, GA side (0.0<Bicl. score<0.5)	301,141	5,661,168
= **Total**	**518,836**	**12,201,497**

Table 2 Data (EN|GA) for back-translation

In Table 2 we give an overview of the monolingual data used for back-translation (see Section 2.4). The English monolingual corpus consists of the English side of the EN–FR *DCEP, DGT, EAC, ECDC* and *JRC-Acquis* corpora. The last corpus is related to the legal domain, while the other corpora serve as generic data for this test case.

The Irish monolingual corpus consists of data extracted from Irish Wikipedia articles and the Irish side of the ParaCrawl corpus (sentences with a Bicleaner score greater than 0 and smaller than 0.5). Imposing a Bicleaner threshold equal to 0 ensures that non-Irish sentences and noisy sentences in general are excluded.

Sentences from the monolingual corpora overlapping with the English or Irish side of the test sets were excluded.

2.2 Machine translation

Neural MT engines were trained with OpenNMT-tensorflow[19] using the Transformer architecture during 20 epochs and default training settings.[20] Preprocessing was done with aggressive tokenization, and joint subword (BPE) and vocabulary sizes set to 32k. NMT systems were trained in both translation directions, EN→GA and GA→EN. The translation quality of the MT models is measured by calculating BLEU scores on two held out test sets (see Section 2.1). The reported BLEU score is the maximal BLEU reached in the last 10 epochs of training.

2.3 Bicleaner

Bicleaner detects noisy sentence pairs in a parallel corpus by estimating the likelihood of a pair of sentences being mutual translations (value near 1) or not (value near 0). Very noisy sentences are given the score 0 and detected by means of hand-crafted hard rules. This set of hand-crafted rules tries to detect evident flaws such as language errors, encoding errors, short segments and very different lengths in pairs of parallel sentences. In a second step, misalignments are detected by means of an automatic classifier. Finally, sentences are scored based on fluency and diversity. More details are provided by Sánchez-Cartagena et al. (2018).

---

[16] https://ec.europa.eu/jrc/en/language-technologies/eac-translation-memory

[17] https://ec.europa.eu/jrc/en/language-technologies/ecdc-translation-memory

[18] http://opus.nlpl.eu/JRC-Acquis.php

[19] https://github.com/OpenNMT/OpenNMT-tf

[20] https://github.com/OpenNMT/OpenNMT-tf/blob/master/opennmt/models/catalog.py

In order to clean the EN–GA web-crawled corpus and the synthetic data obtained via back-translation we used a pre-trained classifier provided by the authors.[21]

2.4 Back-translation

Following the methodology described by Sennrich et al. (2016), we paired EN|GA monolingual data (see Table 2) with EN→GA and GA→EN back-translated data, respectively, and used it as additional synthetic parallel training data.

Our MT engines for back-translation were trained using the RNN (Recurrent Neural Network) architecture in OpenNMT (Klein et al. 2017) on the parallel data described in Table 1. The RNN architecture was chosen because of higher inference speed compared to the Transformer architecture (Vaswani et al. 2017; Zhang et al. 2018), which speeds up the process of back-translation.

We applied Bicleaner to the resulting synthetic parallel corpus in an effort to filter out data that may harm the performance of an NMT engine.

3 Results

Neural MT engines (see Section 2.2) were trained on the different types of training data described in Section 2.1. We evaluated our MT systems on two test sets: a generic test set and a domain-specific test set related to the legal domain. In Table 3 we give an overview of the results. It shows the results of the generic test sets in the third and fifth column and the results for the domain-specific test sets in the fourth and sixth column. In the left column, the types of data are indicated, such as synthetic data obtained after back-translation.

Our NMT engines already perform reasonably well in both language directions using the baseline data only. An increase in BLEU score is observed when adding the web-crawled data and the ParaCrawl data: on the generic test set our results become on par with Google Translate™ in both language directions, while on the domain-specific test set our results are clearly better in terms of BLEU score.

We note that Google Translate™ uses the Google Neural Machine Translation system (Wu et al. 2016) for translating from English into Irish and vice versa. We use Google Translate™, being an open-domain translator, merely as a benchmark.

Adding monolingual data paired with back-translated data (see Section 2.4) to the parallel training corpus resulted in mixed outcomes depending on the translation direction: for EN→GA a small decrease in performance was observed on both test sets, while for GA→EN an increase of almost 4 BLEU was observed on the generic test set. A possible explanation for this may be found in the different nature of the EN and GA monolingual data. The GA monolingual data, consisting of *Wikipedia* and *ParaCrawl,* is less relevant for the domain of our test sets, compared to the EN monolingual data consisting of data closely related to the generic and domain-specific test set.

Type of data	#unique sentence pairs	EN→GA generic	EN→GA domain-sp.	GA→EN generic	GA→EN domain-sp.
Baseline	316k	36.2	52.1	45.4	62.3
+ web-crawled	447k	42.5	59.4	52.6	68.1
+ web-crawled + ParaCrawl	1,189k	44.9	63.5	55.2	71.9
+ web-crawled + ParaCrawl + GA→EN back-translation, Bicleaner score > 0.7	1,414k	44.3	63.0	/	/
+ web-crawled + ParaCrawl + EN→GA back-translation, Bicleaner score > 0.7	3,111k	/	/	59.0	71.1
Google Translate™	/	45.3	49.3	55.3	65.3

Table 3 BLEU scores of our NMT systems for different test sets and types of training data

---

[21] https://github.com/bitextor/bitextor-data/releases/download/bicleaner-v1.0/en-ga.tar.gz

As mentioned in Section 2.4, we applied Bicleaner to the resulting synthetic parallel corpus obtained after back-translation. In order to investigate the effect of this filtering strategy, another set of experiments was performed, for two translation directions.

Table 4 shows the results of two experiments for EN→GA. In the first experiment (second row), an engine was trained on the concatenation of the baseline data, the web-crawled data, the ParaCrawl data and the synthetic parallel corpus; no Bicleaner filtering was applied. In the second experiment, the Bicleaner threshold was set at 0.7. We observe that adding filtered synthetic data results in slightly higher BLEU scores on the domain-specific test set, compared to the scenario in which no filtering was applied. On the generic test set, filtering of the synthetic data did not impact the translation quality in terms of BLEU score.

Table 5 shows the results of a similar set of experiments for GA→EN. Various amounts of synthetic data, filtered with various Bicleaner thresholds, were added to the parallel data. In the second and third row of the table, we show results for the case where only domain-specific data (legal, i.e. back-translation of the *JRC-Acquis* corpus) was used for back-translation. The other experiments used the domain-specific monolingual data and a sample of the other EN monolingual data (i.e. *DCEP, DGT, EAC, ECDC*) for back-translation. In all our experiments, we observed an increase in BLEU score for the generic test set when adding synthetic data to the parallel training corpus. The performance on the domain-specific test set only slightly increases, but only when domain-specific data is used for back-translation, in all other cases a slight decrease is observed. On the generic test set, we found that adding a larger amount of synthetic data results in better performance. However, doubling the amount of training data through back-translation seems sufficient: we only notice small improvements in terms of BLEU score when synthetic data is added beyond the 1:1 ratio between synthetic and real data. This is in line with Poncelas et al. (2018) and Fadaee et al. (2018), who show that a ratio around 1:1 between synthetic and real data is optimal.

Filtering the synthetic data using a misalignment detection tool seems to be a useful strategy in terms of data selection, as slightly higher BLEU scores could be obtained with less data. We refer to the last three rows of Table 5: when using approximately 500k less synthetic sentence pairs, we observe an increase in BLEU of 0.4 on the generic test set (59.0 vs. 58.6). However, we note that one must be careful when setting the Bicleaner threshold: we observe a decrease in BLEU score when increasing the threshold to 0.8.

Type of data	#synthetic sentence pairs before filtering	#unique sentence pairs, total	%synthetic data in total	EN→GA generic	EN→GA domain-sp.
Baseline + web-crawled + ParaCrawl	0k	1,189k	0%	44.9	63.5
+ GA(mono)→EN, no Bicl. threshold	518k	1,708k	30%	44.4	62.0
+ GA(mono)→EN, Bicl. score > 0.7	518k	1,414k	15%	44.3	63.0

Table 4 BLEU scores for EN→GA, given various Bicleaner thresholds for filtering synthetic data

Type of data	#synthetic before filtering	#unique	%synthetic	GA→EN generic	GA→EN domain-sp.
Baseline + web-crawled + ParaCrawl	0k	1,189k	0%	55.2	71.9
+ EN(mono, domain-sp.)→GA, no Bicl. threshold	463k	1,652k	28%	57.5	**72.3**
+ EN(mono, domain-sp.)→GA, Bicl. score >0.7	463k	1,564k	24%	57.4	72.0
+ EN(mono, domain-sp.+generic)→GA, no Bicl. thres.	1,463k	2,652k	54%	58.4	71.3
+ EN(mono, domain-sp.+generic)→GA, Bicl. score >0.7	1,463k	2,338k	48%	58.6	71.6
+ EN(mono, domain-sp.+generic)→GA, Bicl. score >0.8	1,463k	1,997k	40%	58.4	71.7
+ EN(mono, domain-sp.+generic)→GA, no Bicl. thres.	2,463k	3,652k	67%	58.6	70.6
+ EN(mono, domain-sp.+generic)→GA, Bicl. score >0.7	2,463k	3,111k	62%	**59.0**	71.1
+ EN(mono, domain-sp.+generic)→GA, Bicl. score >0.8	2,463k	2,536k	53%	58.3	71.4

Table 5 BLEU scores GA→EN, various amounts of synthetic data and Bicleaner thresholds

4   Conclusion and future work

In this paper we present a well-performing NMT system for the EN–GA language pair. While EN→GA NMT systems presented in previous work (Dowling et al. 2018) were still performing sub-par, our NMT system outperforms Google Translate™ by several BLEU points on a domain-specific test set in both translation directions.

By carefully adding web-crawled data, we were able to increase the training corpus from 316k sentence pairs to more than 1M parallel sentences, leading to better translation performance in terms of BLEU score. In previous studies (Dowling et al. 2015; Arcan et al. 2016), EN↔GA MT systems were trained on significantly smaller corpora.

Next, we showed that back-translation can increase the performance of EN↔GA NMT systems. For the GA→EN translation direction, back-translation proved very useful, especially when EN monolingual data closely related to the domain of the test set was used for back-translation, in line with Sennrich et al. (2016). For the EN→GA translation direction, back-translation proved less effective. We think this might be solved by using Irish monolingual data that is more closely related to the domain of interest. Such data is, to the best of our knowledge, not publicly available. The Corpus of Contemporary Irish, a monolingual collection of Irish-language texts in digital format,[22] containing around 24.7M words, may be a possible candidate. However, this corpus is only searchable and we could therefore not use it in the present study.

Finally, we presented a lightweight method for filtering synthetic sentence pairs obtained via back-translation, using a tool for misalignment detection, Bicleaner (Sánchez-Cartagena et al. 2018). We show that our approach results in small increases in BLEU score, while requiring less training data.

In future work we will investigate to what extent our proposed methodology can be applied to other languages with a similar amount of data available. Another interesting research direction would be the development of a multilingual MT system which includes not only Irish but also other Gaelic languages, and which is based on methods such as the one described by Johnson et al. (2016). It should also be investigated whether unsupervised MT approaches like the one of Lample et al. (2019) can be used to increase the translation quality of EN↔GA MT systems.

Acknowledgement

This work was performed in the framework of the SMART 2015/1091 project ("Tools and resources for CEF automated translation"), funded by the CEF Telecom programme (Connecting Europe Facility).

References

Mihael Arcan, Caoilfhionn Lane, Eoin Ó Droighneáin and Paul Buitelaar. 2016. *Iris: English-Irish Machine Translation System*. Proceedings of LREC 10, pages 566–572.

Amittai Axelrod, Xiaodong He and Jianfeng Gao. 2011. *Domain Adaptation via Pseudo In-domain Data Selection*. Proceedings of the 2011 Conference on Empirical Methods in Natural Language Processing. Association for Computational Linguistics, pages 355–362.

Meghan Dowling, Lauren Cassidy, Eimear Maguire, Teresa Lynn, Ankit Srivastava and John Judge. 2015. *Tapadóir: Developing a Statistical Machine Translation Engine and Associated Resources for Irish*. Proceedings of The Fourth LRL Workshop: "Language Technologies in support of Less-Resourced Languages", Poznan, Poland.

Meghan Dowling, Teresa Lynn, Alberto Poncelas and Andy Way. 2018. *SMT versus NMT: Preliminary Comparisons for Irish*. Proceedings of AMTA 2018 Workshop: LoResMT 2018, pages 12–20.

Marzieh Fadaee and Christof Monz. 2018. *Back-translation Sampling by Targeting Difficult Words in Neural Machine Translation*. Proceedings of the 2018 Conference on Empirical Methods in Natural Language Processing. Association for Computational Linguistics, pages 436–446.

Thanh-Le Ha, Jan Niehues and Alexander Waibel. 2016. *Toward Multilingual Neural Machine Translation with Universal Encoder and Decoder*. Proceedings of the 13th International Workshop on Spoken Language Translation (IWSLT).

Najeh Hajlaoui, David Kolovratnik, Jaakko Väyrynen, Ralf Steinberger and Daniel Varga. 2014. *DCEP – Digital Corpus of the European Parliament*. Proceedings of LREC 9, pages 3164–3171.

Aizhan Imankulova, Takayuki Sato and Mamoru Komachi. 2017. *Improving Low-resource Neural Machine Translation with Filtered Pseudo-parallel Corpus*. Proceedings of the 4th Workshop on Asian Translation, pages 70–78.

---

[22] https://www.gaois.ie/g3m/en

Melvin Johnson, Mike Schuster, Quoc V. Le, Maxim Krikun, Yonghui Wu, Zhifeng Chen, Nikhil Thorat, Fernanda Viégas, Martin Wattenberg, Greg Corrado, Macduff Hughes and Jeffrey Dean. 2016. Google's Multilingual Neural Machine Translation System: Enabling Zero-Shot Translation. In *Transactions of the Association for Computational Linguistics* 5, pages 339–351.

John Judge, Ailbhe Ní Chasaide, Rose Ní Dhubhda, Kevin P. Scannell and Elaine Uí Dhonnchadha. 2012. An Ghaeilge sa Ré Dhigiteach – The Irish Language in the Digital Age. In *META-NET White Paper Series*. Georg Rehm and Hans Uszkoreit (Series Editors). Springer. Available online at *http://www.meta-net.eu/whitepapers*.

Huda Khayrallah and Philipp Koehn. 2018. *On the Impact of Various Types of Noise on Neural Machine Translation*. Proceedings of the 2nd Workshop on Neural Machine Translation. Association for Computational Linguistics, pages 74–83.

Guillaume Klein, Yoon Kim, Yuntian Deng, Jean Senellart and Alexander M. Rush. 2017. *OpenNMT: Open-Source Toolkit for Neural Machine Translation*. https://arxiv.org/abs/1701.02810.

Philipp Koehn and Rebecca Knowles. 2017. *Six Challenges for Neural Machine Translation*. Proceedings of the First Workshop on Neural Machine Translation, pages 28–39.

Guillaume Lample and Alexis Conneau. 2019. *Cross-lingual Language Model Pretraining*. https://arxiv.org/abs/1901.07291

Alberto Poncelas, Dimitar Shterionov, Andy Way, Gideon Maillette de Buy Wenniger and Peyman Passban. 2018. *Investigating Backtranslation in Neural Machine Translation*. https://arxiv.org/abs/1804.06189

Víctor M. Sánchez-Cartagena, Marta Bañón, Sergio Ortiz-Rojas and Gema Ramírez-Sánchez. 2018. *Prompsit's Submission to WMT 2018 Parallel Corpus Filtering Shared Task*. Proceedings of WMT18, Volume 2: Shared Task Papers, pages 995–962.

Rico Sennrich, Barry Haddow and Alexandra Birch. 2016. *Improving Neural Machine Translation Models with Monolingual Data*. Proceedings of the 54th Annual Meeting of the Association for Computational Linguistics (Volume 1: Long Papers), Berlin, Germany. Association for Computational Linguistics, pages 86–96.

Marlies van der Wees, Arianna Bisazza and Christof Monz. 2017. *Dynamic Data Selection for Neural Machine Translation*. Proceedings of the 2017 Conference on Emperical Methods in Natural Language Processing, Copenhagen, Denmark.

Association for Computational Lunguistics, pages 1400–1410.

Daniel Varga, László Németh, Péter Halácsy, András Kornai, Viktor Trón and Viktor Nagy. 2005. *Parallel Corpora for Medium Density Languages*. Proceedings of RANLP 2005, pages 590–596.

Ashish Vaswani, Noam Shazeer, Niki Parmar, Jakob Uszkoreit, Lilion Jones, Aidan N. Gomez, Łukasz Kaiser and Illia Polosukhin. 2017. *Attention is All You Need*. Proceedings of 31st Conference on Neural Information Processing Systems (NIPS 2017), pages 5998–6008.

Yonghui Wu, Mike Schuster, Zhifeng Chen, Quoc V. Le, Mohammad Norouzi, Wolfgang Macherey et al. 2016. *Google's Neural Machine Translation System: Bridging the Gap between Human and Machine Translation*. arxiv.org/abs/1609.08144

Biao Zhang, Deyi Xiong and Jinsong Su. 2018. *Accelerating Neural Transformer via an Average Attention Network*. Proceedings of the 56th Annual Meeting of the Association for Computational Linguistics (Long Papers), pages 1789–1798.

Sentence-Level Adaptation for Low-Resource Neural Machine Translation

Aaron Mueller* and **Yash Kumar Lal***
Center for Language & Speech Processing
Department of Computer Science
Johns Hopkins University
{amueller,ykumar}@jhu.edu

Abstract

Current neural machine translation (NMT) approaches achieve state-of-the-art accuracy in high-resource contexts. However, NMT requires a great deal of parallel data to deliver acceptable results; thus, it is currently unsuited for translating in low-resource contexts (especially when compared to phrase-based approaches). We propose a method that better leverages the limited data available in such low-resource settings by adapting the model for each sentence at inference time. A general NMT model is trained on the limited training data; then, for each test sentence, its parameters are fine-tuned over a subset of similar sentences extracted from the training set. We experiment with various similarity metrics to extract these similar sentences. It is observed that the sentence-adapted models achieve slightly increased BLEU scores compared to standard neural approaches on a Xhosa-English dataset.

1 Introduction

Neural machine translation (NMT) (Bahdanau et al., 2014) has become the primary paradigm in machine translation literature. NMT aims to learn an end-to-end neural model to optimize translation performance by generalizing machine translation as a sequence-to-sequence machine learning problem.

The first NMT systems (Sutskever et al., 2014; Kalchbrenner and Blunsom, 2013) were built with recurrent neural networks based on encoder-decoder architectures. Bahdanau et al. (2014) and Luong et al. (2015) proposed the use of attention mechanisms to translate better by considering the context in which particular target words occur with respect to the source contexts. Recently, transformers (Vaswani et al., 2017) have been shown to achieve state-of-the-art performance across various high-resource language pairs.

The strength of this approach lies in processing large amounts of parallel data and quickly learning from aligned translations without pre-defined linguistic rules. NMT directly models the probability of a target-language sentence given aligned source- and target-language sentences and does not need to train separate language models and alignment models like statistical machine translation (SMT) (Koehn et al., 2003; Chiang, 2005). The unavailability of large parallel corpora for most language pairs, however, is a ubiquitous problem. These are only available for a handful of resource-rich languages, and in limited domains such as news reports or parliamentary/congressional proceedings.

Neural approaches to MT in general are data-hungry and therefore tend to perform inadequately in low-resource contexts (Koehn and Knowles, 2017). Thus, improving NMT for low-resource languages has been a topic of recent interest. While unsupervised NMT (Artetxe et al., 2018) has been suggested to reduce NMT's need for aligned translations, it does not perform effectively for low-resource languages (Guzmán et al., 2019). Present practices in the domain leverage the strength of preliminary word-level translation models, which do not work well. However, transfer learning from high-resource parallel datasets (Zoph et al., 2016), as well as data augmentation through pivot corpora (Choi et al., 2018), trans-

* Equal contribution.

lating monolingual data (Zhang and Zong, 2016), and/or copying data from source to target side (Currey et al., 2017) have proven effective in such cases.

Our method attempts to better leverage limited data by adapting parameters for each sentence at inference time. This is carried out by fine-tuning (Sennrich et al., 2015; Luong and Manning, 2015b) the parameters of an NMT model over a subset of training sentences which are similar to a given test sentence. By contrast, existing NMT systems tend to employ parameters which are unchanged for any given test sentence after training or continued training (Luong and Manning, 2015a).

There exists evidence that customising an NMT model for each test sentence gives it a better chance of producing correct translations (Wuebker et al., 2018). In our model, for every test sentence, a unique subset of similar training sentences is retrieved. This training-sentence subset is used to fine-tune the base model at inference time. We experiment with string-based similarity and representation-based similarity to retrieve similar sentences; precision, recall, and Levenshtein distance are used for the former, and cosine similarity on word embeddings is used for the latter. A combination of these is used to create the final subset of similar sentences.

2 Related Work

In statistical machine translation, Liu et al. (2012) proposed a local training method to learn sentence-wise weights for different test sentences. Due to the relatively lower number of weights in SMT, fine-tuning them does not fully exploit similar sentences. Koehn and Senellart (2010; Ma et al. (2011; Bertoldi and Federico (2013; Wang et al. (2013) carefully designed features to generate similar sentences and use them in the translation memory. These methods worked when the similarity of the test sentence and the sentences in the similar subset was reasonably high. Moore and Lewis (2010) proposed selecting non-domain-specific language model (LM) training data by comparing its cross-entropy with as domain-specific LM, while Duh et al. (2013) used neural LMs for adaptation data selection.

Domain adaptation (Ben-David et al., 2010; Chu and Wang, 2018) can be applied in order to learn from a source-language distribution a well performing model on a different (but related) target data distribution. Continued training (Luong and Manning, 2015a) is a commonly applied technique in domain adaptation where a general NMT system is trained on a large amounts of out-of-domain parallel data; then, the general model is adapted for a particular domain. Sentence-level adaptation is analogous to the problem of domain adaptation if each sentence is considered its own domain, and we therefore consider the sentence adaptation task a subset of the domain adaptation task. Our approach is similar to the more fine-grained document-level adaptation of Kothur et al. (2018), though we adapt on multiple complete sentences rather than populating a dictionary of novel-word translations or adapting on the previous sentence. Farajian et al. (2017) work on translations in multiple domains by generating instance-based adaptation hyperparameters in an unsupervised fashion.

Li et al. (2016) present a dynamic NMT approach where the general NMT model is adapted per-sentence; however, they adapt on only a single similar sentence and employ their system in a high-resource context. We propose additional similarity metrics and adapt on multiple similar sentences obtained from each metric. The pipeline employed here is similar to that of Zhang et al. (2018), where "translation pieces" are extracted to improve translations for particular sentences. However, their approach uses only lexical measures of similarity—edit distance and similar n-grams—and relies on these similar lexical features as opposed to entire sentences from the training corpus. Our system employs lexical, character-based, and embedding-based similarities to retrieve sentences, making it better suited for the task.

3 Model Architecture

We discuss the various components of our proposed approach in detail. An overview of the architecture can be found in Figure 1.

3.1 Transformer

Recently, transformers (Vaswani et al., 2017) have proven highly effective in machine translation; as they process each word, self-attention allows them to peek at other positions in the input sequence itself to create a better encoding. We employ transformers as the foundation for our model.

The transformer encoder is composed of 2 sublayers: self-attention and a feedforward network.

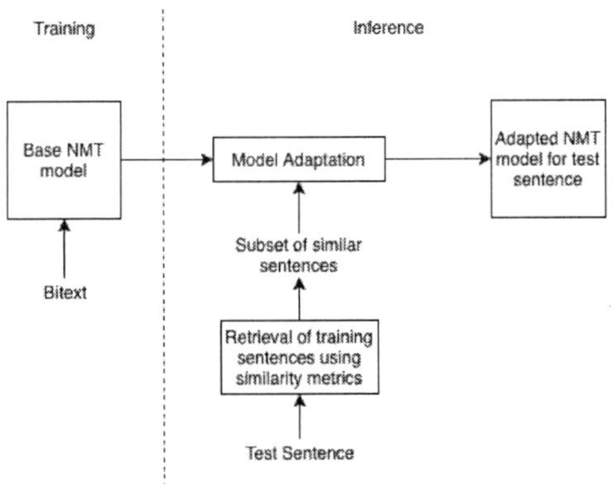

Figure 1: Architecture overview.

First, the input is used to create query, key, and value vectors. Vaswani et al. (2017) extend the dot product attention described in Luong et al. (2015) to consider these vectors. Self-attention is further refined into multi-head attention, allowing the model to focus on different parts of the input sequence at once.

Self-attention in the decoder is applied as it is in the encoder. However, the attention on future time steps is masked out to prevent from attending to future positions. The output embeddings in the decoder are offset by one position. Both of these modifications combined ensure that model predictions for any position can depend only on known outputs of previous positions. Such blocks can be stacked to form multi-layer encoders and decoders.

3.2 Similarity Metrics

Our method consists of adapting a base NMT model over a small set of relevant sentences for refinement of its parameters.

We employ four types of similarity metrics (eight total metrics) to retrieve sentences from the training set that are similar to a given test sentence. The first of these is character-based Levenshtein distance:

$$distance = subs + dels + inserts \qquad (1)$$

The sentences which return the minimum distance from the test sentence are considered to be the most similar and are added to the fine-tuning subset. We expect that this metric may capture similar subwords.

Our second and third metric types employ lexical similarities between sentences. We take inspiration from BLEU (Papineni et al., 2002), which

is a modified n-gram precision between a reference and generated translation. To capture lexical similarity, we count unigram, bigram, or trigram matches, then normalize over the number of n-grams in the test sentence (for recall) and the number of n-grams in the candidate sentence from the training set (for precision):

$$precision = \frac{count_{match}(train, test)}{count(ngrams \in train)} \qquad (2)$$

$$recall = \frac{count_{match}(train, test)}{count(ngrams \in test)} \qquad (3)$$

In Equations 2 and 3, $count_{match}$ refers to the number of matching n-grams between the sentence to be inferred ($test$) and a candidate sentence from the training set ($train$). Note that we employ three different n-gram orders (unigram, bigram, trigram) for both of these metric types, yielding six total precision- and recall-based similarity metrics.

Our fourth metric type attempts to capture semantic similarity between sentences. For this, we calculate the cosine similarity across two sentences as follows:

$$cos(\theta) = \frac{s_1 \cdot s_2}{||s_1|| \cdot ||s_2||} \qquad (4)$$

Here, vectors s_1 and s_2 are the mean word embeddings (Mikolov et al., 2013) for sentence 1 and sentence 2, respectively:

$$s = \frac{\sum_{w \in W} w}{|s|} \qquad (5)$$

where w is a word embedding, W is the list of all word embeddings in a given sentence s, and $|s|$ is the length of the sentence in tokens. The sum and division are element-wise operations which yield a vector of the same length as any given w in W. Although simple, it has been demonstrated that this is a strong method to generate sentence embeddings (Arora et al., 2017).

Each metric (precision and recall of different n-gram orders account for six out of the eight distinct metrics) contributes 11 sentences[1] each to the final adaptation subset. We present a list of similar sentences retrieved by each metric for a sample test sentence in Table 6.

Since each of the metrics is calculated against all training sentences, this approach is more suited for a low-resource setting rather than a high-resource one.

---

[1]This is an arbitrarily chosen number.

	Sentence	Eng Words	Xhosa Words
Train	20544	614441	388778
Test	1956	58323	36700
Dev	1956	59140	37353

Table 1: English-Xhosa Bible dataset at a glance.

α_A	BLEU
0.0001	22.51
0.0004	**22.83**
0.00045	22.82
0.0005	22.82
0.0006	22.59
0.00075	22.26
0.001	19.12

Table 2: Learning rate during adaptation (α_A) vs. BLEU scores in the Xhosa→English translation task. Note: $\alpha_T = 0.0005$.

3.3 Inference-Time Adaptation

Our pipeline is split into two stages. First, network parameters are calculated by training over the entire training corpus; this is denoted as θ. This corresponds to the training stage of Figure 1. Second, the parameters θ are modified slightly to increase the log-likelihood over the subset of sentences which are similar to the test sentence (that are extracted using the similarity metrics in Section 3.2). The modified parameters are denoted as $\hat{\theta}$. This is formalized as follows:

$$\hat{\theta} = \arg\max_{\theta} \left(\log \prod_{S^{(k)} \sim S} p(T^{(k)} | S^{(k)}; \theta) \right) \quad (6)$$

where S denotes the source-language corpus of similar sentences, T denotes the target-language corpus of similar sentences, $S^{(k)}$ and $T^{(k)}$ denote the kth sentence in the aligned corpus, and $\hat{\theta}$ refers to the network parameters of the adapted model. These computations[2] occur in the inference stage of Figure 1.

4 Experiments

4.1 Data

We translate Xhosa—a true low-resource language—to English, employing translated

Bibles as our dataset (Christodouloupoulos and Steedman, 2015).[3] Dataset statistics are available in Table 1. We work with word-level data for our experiments.

Xhosa is a Niger-Congo language spoken by approximately 8 million native speakers and 11 million L2 speakers (Lewis, 2015). Relative to English, it is a synthetic language with a rich morpheme inventory (Oosthuysen, 2016). Due to Xhosa's synthetic morphology, its English translations often demonstrate one-to-many relations; i.e., one Xhosa word will often translate as multiple English words, which explains the disparity between the number of Xhosa tokens and English tokens in our dataset.

4.2 Training Details

All neural models herein are trained with Sockeye (Hieber et al., 2017).

For each of the similarity metrics, we retrieve the most similar sentences and concatenate them into a single dataset, generating a total adaptation subset of 88 sentences for each test sentence (11 per metric). As the adaptation dataset is small compared to the training corpus, special care is needed to optimize strategic overfitting during inference; we therefore restrict adaptation to just one epoch.

4.2.1 Adaptation Learning Rate Experiments

The learning rate for adaptation α_A essentially dictates how much fine-tuning the NMT system receives during adaptation. Each language has a different ideal adaptation rate, so we perform a sweep and report our findings in Table 2.

It is clear that trying to learn very aggressively from the adaptation subset results in a decrease in performance. Trying to adjust the weights of the network too much with respect to the loss function might result in disregarding some local minima from consideration, resulting in an adverse effect. It is also found that setting α_A too low also results in a slight score decrease, so finding the optimal α_A is crucial. It is observed that, in this case, an α_A of 0.0004 best suits our objective. Note that this is similar to the training learning rate α_T of 0.0005, and that the other best-performing α_A values are similar to α_T as well.

---

[2] Note that we pre-compute similar sentences before running inference; this saves time when translating sentences at test time. We do not peek at or manually modify the similar sentences for any test sentence.

[3] Religious texts are often the first to be translated into a given language. Translated Bibles are therefore available for many low-resource language varieties.

Base Model	Unadapted	$\alpha_A = .0004$	$\alpha_A = .0005$
LSTM (Luong et al., 2015)	20.73	-	-
Transformer ($\alpha_T = .0001$) (Vaswani et al., 2017)	20.52	-	17.74
Transformer ($\alpha_T = .0005$) (Vaswani et al., 2017)	**22.76**	**22.83**	22.82

Table 3: Evaluation of Xhosa→English translation systems.

src	Wathi uThixo , Makubekho isibhakabhaka phakathi kwawo amanzi , sibe ngumahlulo wokwahlula amanzi kumanzi .
ref	And God said , Let there be a firmament in the midst of the waters , and let it divide the waters from the waters .
no adaptation	And God said , Let there be clouds in the midst of them , let the water of the morning to the water .
w/ adaptation	And God said , Let there be clouds *in the midst of the waters* to *divide the water from the waters* .
src	Wathi uYehova uThixo kumfazi , Yintoni na le nto uyenzileyo ? Wathi umfazi , Inyoka indilukuhlile , ndadla ke .
ref	And the LORD God said unto the woman , What is this that thou hast done ? And the woman said , The serpent beguiled me , and I did eat .
no adaptation	*And the LORD God said unto the woman* , What hast thou done this thing ? And she said , I have eaten the wife , and did eat .
w/ adaptation	*And the LORD God said unto the woman* , What hast thou done ? And the woman said , I have eaten , and did eat .

Table 4: Sample translations comparing unadapted and adapted output. Notably poor translations are highlighted in red bold, whereas notably good translations are highlighted in *blue italics*.

Metric	Unadapted	Adapted
Unigram Match %	53.9	54.1
Bigram Match %	28.4	28.5
Trigram Match %	16.7	16.7
4-gram Match %	10.5	10.6
Brevity Penalty	1.000	1.000

Table 5: Investigation of the constituent features of our BLEU scores for Xhosa→English translations.

4.3 Baselines

We focus on comparing the performance of neural models, as this work extends NMT for low-resource contexts.

The first neural model against which we evaluate our approach is the standard encoder-decoder architecture with recurrent units. The encoder units are bidirectional LSTMs (Schuster and Paliwal, 1997) while the decoder unit incorporates an LSTM (Hochreiter and Schmidhuber, 1997) with dot product attention (Luong et al., 2015). The model was trained with a word batch size of 1024, with source and target embedding layer size 256 and hidden layer size 512. The initial learning rate was set to 0.0001 with a decay factor of 0.9. We impose a dropout rate (Srivastava et al., 2014) of 0.1 and use the Adam optimizer (Kingma and Ba, 2015).

The second baseline is a Transformer architecture. Both the encoder and decoder have two sub-layers employing multi-head attention. The number of heads in this mechanism is 4. Other parameters are kept constant from the LSTM model. As the transformer model outperforms the LSTM (see Table 3), we use it as the base of our adapted model.

5 Results and Evaluation

Table 3 contains all BLEU scores for our unadapted and adapted models. While it may seem beneficial in theory to have α_T be less than α_A, we find empirically that having similar α_T and α_A values results in better BLEU scores. The base transformer trained with a learning rate α_T of 0.0001 performs more poorly compared to that with an α_T of .0005. We therefore focus primarily on models where $\alpha_T = 0.0005$. Both of these trends could be because we are "adapting" on a subset of the data on which we train.

The percentage of n-gram matches (unigram to 4-gram) is higher for the adapted model than the other neural approaches; see Table 5. This suggests that we match more lexical content to the reference translations; this causes increased fluency and semantic similarity. Indeed, our model narrows the lexical matching gap between the baseline transformer and the phrase-based system. This leads to a slight increase in BLEU scores for the generated translations.

Sample translations may be found in Table 4; these were chosen randomly from the output translations. Note that the example translations from the adapted model tend to be more fluent than the translations from the unadapted model due to not including as many non-sequitur tokens.

The adequacy of the adapted translations also seems to be slightly better (or at least no worse): the only non-matching lexical translation in the first sample (*clouds*, as opposed to the reference *firmament*) is semantically close to the reference. Compare to the unadapted model's sentence, whose second clause is semantically unacceptable and bears little resemblance to the reference translation's intended semantic value. Similarly, in the second sentence, the adapted model has a similar non-sequitur translation for the highlighted clause, although the adapted model's translation omits more non-sequitur words to produce a more fluent translation without losing as much adequacy as the unadapted model's translation.

5.1 Qualitative Sentence Similarity Metric Evaluation

To investigate what types of sentences are retrieved by our similarity metrics from Section 3.2, we run a script which retrieves the most similar training sentences (per-metric) for a randomly chosen test sentence in English. The most similar sentences per-metric, as well as their similarity/distance scores, are shown in Table 6. Note that this sentence similarity process is run for only the source language, Xhosa, and that this set of similar sentences in English is retrieved solely to demonstrate what types of sentences these similarity metrics choose in general.

Notably, precision and recall sometimes result in different similar sentences for the same n-gram orders. Unigram precision and unigram recall re-

trieve largely distinct sentences with very different scores, though there is often overlap: unigram recall, bigram precision, and bigram recall return the same sentence as most similar. Trigram precision and recall return similar sentences that are distinct from the previous n-gram orders; the precision and recall sentences are the same in this case, but not always. Thus, using different n-gram orders—and precision as well as recall within each n-gram order—can feasibly return different similar sentences. We thus keep all of these similarity metrics in our similar-sentence subset.

Cosine similarity retrieves a sentence which has a similar general tone to the test sentence, as well as a similar topic (the story of creation), but otherwise the n-grams are quite different. This seems to be beneficial, for it demonstrates that we retrieve sentences which do not necessarily have the same words as the sentence on which we perform inference, but which have commonalities with respect to some supralinguistic or semantic feature(s). This trend also holds for other sentences in the test set for which we retrieved similar sentences, so it does generally seem to return related sentences.

Levenshtein distance, in contrast, does not seem to return a useful similar sentence in this example. There are few n-gram or morphemic matches in common between the test and similar sentences, and the meaning of the retrieved sentence bears little resemblance to that of the test sentence. In general, the Levenshtein distance seems useful in retrieving similar sentences with different inflections of the same words primarily when there exists another sentence with similar unigrams in the same order as the test sentence (i.e., it works primarily when two sentences exist that are already very lexically similar). In the future, it would perhaps it would be more beneficial to run Levenshtein distance on subwords after performing a BPE operation, rather than on characters. As this metric only comprises a small fraction of the similar-sentence subset on which we adapt, it should be inconsequential if some sentences are not particularly relevant from this metric. If they are relevant, however, it will be quite beneficial, so we keep these sentences in our similar-sentence adaptation set regardless.

We observe that sometimes, a sentence with zero or negligible score is also returned by one of the metrics. As an extension, thresholding the

	test sentence	Behold , this is the joy of his way , and out of the earth shall others grow .	
levenshtein distance	And the evening and the morning were the third day .		54
unigram precision	And God said , Let the earth bring forth grass , the herb yielding seed , and the fruit tree yielding fruit after his kind , whose seed is in itself , upon the earth : and it was so .		0.8421
unigram recall	And the earth was without form , and void ; and darkness was upon the face of the deep . And the Spirit of God moved upon the face of the waters .		0.455
bigram precision	And the earth was without form , and void ; and darkness was upon the face of the deep . And the Spirit of God moved upon the face of the waters .		0.222
bigram recall	And the earth was without form , and void ; and darkness was upon the face of the deep . And the Spirit of God moved upon the face of the waters .		0.125
trigram precision	And he shewed me a pure river of water of life , clear as crystal , proceeding out of the throne of God and of the Lamb .		0.059
trigram recall	And he shewed me a pure river of water of life , clear as crystal , proceeding out of the throne of God and of the Lamb .		0.038
cosine similarity	And God said , Let there be light : and there was light .		0.397

Table 6: This table features the most similar sentence retrieved from the training set per similarity metric for an arbitrary test sentence. Note that Levenshtein distance is a distance metric and not a similarity metric, so we retrieve the minimum-distance sentence as opposed to the highest-similarity sentence.

score for each metric when retrieving similar sentences might boost performance since it will only return higher quality matches.

6 Conclusion

We propose an architecture-independent approach to give neural models a better chance of leveraging limited parallel data in low-resource contexts. The model produced by adapting the low-resource NMT model per-sentence generates translations with slightly higher adequacy and seemingly improved fluency; BLEU scores are similar, though in this case slightly higher after adaptation. We note in particular that tuning both the training-time and adaptation-time learning rates is crucial; extensions could therefore test different values in a grid search for linguistically diverse language pairs.

Future work could also refine the similar-sentence adaptation subset and threshold sentences according to some interpolated metric based on all similarity metrics. The flexibility of our approach means that it is easy to integrate other similar algorithms as new similarity metrics. In particular, bilateral multi-perspective matching (Wang et al., 2017) at the sentence level could be of interest.

Another possible extension is to look at subword-level matching criteria for the retrieval component of our approach. One could also study the relative performance of this approach for synthetic vs. analytic languages with different neural model base architectures before adaptation.

References

Arora, Sanjeev, Yingyu Liang, and Tengyu Ma. 2017. A Simple but Tough-to-Beat Baseline for Sentence Embeddings. In *International Conference on Learning Representations*.

Artetxe, Mikel, Gorka Labaka, Eneko Agirre, and Kyunghyun Cho. 2018. Unsupervised Neural Machine Translation. In *International Conference on Learning Representations*.

Bahdanau, Dzmitry, Kyunghyun Cho, and Yoshua Bengio. 2014. Neural Machine Translation by Jointly Learning to Align and Translate. *arXiv preprint arXiv:1409.0473*.

Ben-David, Shai, John Blitzer, Koby Crammer, Alex Kulesza, Fernando Pereira, and Jennifer Vaughan. 2010. A Theory of Learning from Different Domains. *Machine Learning*, 79:151–175.

Bertoldi, N., Cettolo M. and M. Federico. 2013. Cache-based online adaptation for machine translation enhanced computer assisted translation. In *Pro-*

ceedings of the XIV Machine Translation Summit, pages 35–42.

Chiang, David. 2005. A Hierarchical Phrase-based Model for Statistical Machine Translation. In *Proceedings of the 43rd Annual Meeting on Association for Computational Linguistics*, ACL '05, pages 263–270.

Choi, Gyu Hyeon, Jong Hun Shin, and Young Kil Kim. 2018. Improving a Multi-Source Neural Machine Translation Model with Corpus Extension for Low-Resource Languages. In chair), Nicoletta Calzolari (Conference, Khalid Choukri, Christopher Cieri, Thierry Declerck, Sara Goggi, Koiti Hasida, Hitoshi Isahara, Bente Maegaard, Joseph Mariani, Hlne Mazo, Asuncion Moreno, Jan Odijk, Stelios Piperidis, and Takenobu Tokunaga, editors, *Proceedings of the Eleventh International Conference on Language Resources and Evaluation (LREC 2018)*, Miyazaki, Japan, May 7-12, 2018. European Language Resources Association (ELRA).

Christodouloupoulos, Christos and Mark Steedman. 2015. A Massively Parallel Corpus: The Bible in 100 Languages. *Lang. Resour. Eval.*, 49(2):375–395, June.

Chu, Chenhui and Rui Wang. 2018. A Survey of Domain Adaptation for Neural Machine Translation. In *Proceedings of the 27th International Conference on Computational Linguistics*, pages 1304–1319. Association for Computational Linguistics.

Currey, Anna, Antonio Valerio Miceli Barone, and Kenneth Heafield. 2017. Copied Monolingual Data Improves Low-Resource Neural Machine Translation. In *Proceedings of the Second Conference on Machine Translation*, pages 148–156. Association for Computational Linguistics.

Duh, Kevin, Sudoh Katsuhito Neubig, Graham, and Hajime Tsukada. 2013. Adaptation Data Selection using Neural Language Models: Experiments in Machine Translation. In *Proceedings of the 51th Annual Meeting of the Association for Computational Linguistics (Volume 2: Short Papers)*, Sofia, Bulgaria, August. Association for Computational Linguistics.

Farajian, M. Amin, Marco Turchi, Matteo Negri, and Marcello Federico. 2017. Multi-Domain Neural Machine Translation through Unsupervised Adaptation. In *Proceedings of the Second Conference on Machine Translation*, pages 127–137. Association for Computational Linguistics.

Guzmán, Francisco, Peng-Jen Chen, Myle Ott, Juan Pino, Guillaume Lample, Philipp Koehn, Vishrav Chaudhary, and Marc'Aurelio Ranzato. 2019. Two New Evaluation Datasets for Low-Resource Machine Translation: Nepali-English and Sinhala-English. *arXiv preprint arXiv:1902.01382*.

Hieber, Felix, Tobias Domhan, Michael Denkowski, David Vilar, Artem Sokolov, Ann Clifton, and Matt Post. 2017. Sockeye: A Toolkit for Neural Machine Translation. *CoRR*, abs/1712.05690.

Hochreiter, Sepp and Jürgen Schmidhuber. 1997. Long Short-term Memory. *Neural computation*, 9(8):1735–1780.

Kalchbrenner, Nal and Phil Blunsom. 2013. Recurrent Continuous Translation Models. In *Proceedings of the 2013 Conference on Empirical Methods in Natural Language Processing*, pages 1700–1709. Association for Computational Linguistics.

Kingma, Diederik P. and Jimmy Ba. 2015. Adam: A Method for Stochastic Optimization. In *Proceedings of the 3rd International Conference on Learning Representations (ICLR)*.

Koehn, Philipp and Rebecca Knowles. 2017. Six Challenges for Neural Machine Translation. In *Proceedings of the First Workshop on Neural Machine Translation*, pages 28–39. Association for Computational Linguistics.

Koehn, Philipp and Jean Senellart. 2010. Convergence of Translation Memory and Statistical Machine Translation. In *Proceedings of AMTA Workshop on MT Research and the Translation Industry*, pages 21–31, Denver.

Koehn, Philipp, Franz Josef Och, and Daniel Marcu. 2003. Statistical Phrase-based Translation. In *Proceedings of the 2003 Conference of the North American Chapter of the Association for Computational Linguistics on Human Language Technology - Volume 1*, NAACL '03, pages 48–54.

Kothur, Sachith Sri Ram, Rebecca Knowles, and Philipp Koehn. 2018. Document-Level Adaptation for Neural Machine Translation. In *Proceedings of the 2nd Workshop on Neural Machine Translation and Generation*, pages 64–73. Association for Computational Linguistics.

Lewis, M. Paul, editor. 2015. *Ethnologue: Languages of the World*. SIL International, Dallas, TX, USA, eighteenth edition.

Li, Xiaoqing, Jiajun Zhang, and Chengqing Zong. 2016. One Sentence One Model for Neural Machine Translation. *CoRR*, abs/1609.06490.

Liu, Lemao, Hailong Cao, Taro Watanabe, Tiejun Zhao, Mo Yu, and CongHui Zhu. 2012. Locally Training the Log-linear Model for SMT. In *Proceedings of the 2012 Joint Conference on Empirical Methods in Natural Language Processing and Computational Natural Language Learning*, EMNLP-CoNLL '12, pages 402–411.

Luong, Minh-Thang and Christopher D. Manning. 2015a. Neural Machine Translation Systems for Spoken Language Domains. In *International Workshop on Spoken Language Translation*.

Luong, Minh-Thang and Christopher D. Manning. 2015b. Stanford Neural Machine Translation Systems for Spoken Language Domain. In *International Workshop on Spoken Language Translation*, Da Nang, Vietnam.

Luong, Minh-Thang, Hieu Pham, and Christopher D Manning. 2015. Effective Approaches to Attention-based Neural Machine Translation. *arXiv preprint arXiv:1508.04025*.

Ma, Yanjun, Yifan He, Andy Way, and Josef van Genabith. 2011. Consistent Translation Using Discriminative Learning: A Translation Memory-inspired Approach. In *Proceedings of the 49th Annual Meeting of the Association for Computational Linguistics: Human Language Technologies - Volume 1*, HLT '11, pages 1239–1248.

Mikolov, Tomas, Ilya Sutskever, Kai Chen, Greg Corrado, and Jeffrey Dean. 2013. Distributed Representations of Words and Phrases and their Compositionality. In *Advances in Neural Information Processing Systems*.

Moore, Robert C. and William Lewis. 2010. Intelligent Selection of Language Model Training Data. In *Proceedings of the ACL 2010 Conference Short Papers*, ACLShort '10, pages 220–224, Stroudsburg, PA, USA. Association for Computational Linguistics.

Oosthuysen, JC. 2016. *The Grammar of isiXhosa*. African Sun Media, Stellenbosch, South Africa.

Papineni, Kishore, Salim Roukos, Todd Ward, and Wei-Jing Zhu. 2002. BLEU: A Method for Automatic Evaluation of Machine Translation. In *Proceedings of the 40th Annual Meeting on Association for Computational Linguistics*, ACL '02, pages 311–318.

Schuster, Mike and Kuldip K Paliwal. 1997. Bidirectional Recurrent Neural Networks. *IEEE Transactions on Signal Processing*, 45(11):2673–2681.

Sennrich, Rico, Barry Haddow, and Alexandra Birch. 2015. Improving neural machine translation models with monolingual data. *arXiv preprint arXiv:1511.06709*.

Srivastava, Nitish, Geoffrey Hinton, Alex Krizhevsky, Ilya Sutskever, and Ruslan Salakhutdinov. 2014. Dropout: A Simple Way to Prevent Neural Networks from Overfitting. *J. Mach. Learn. Res.*, pages 1929–1958.

Sutskever, Ilya, Oriol Vinyals, and Quoc V Le. 2014. Sequence to sequence learning with neural networks. In *Advances in neural information processing systems*, pages 3104–3112.

Vaswani, Ashish, Noam Shazeer, Niki Parmar, Jakob Uszkoreit, Llion Jones, Aidan N Gomez, Ł ukasz Kaiser, and Illia Polosukhin. 2017. Attention is All You Need. In *Advances in Neural Information Processing Systems*, pages 5998–6008.

Wang, Kun, Chengqing Zong, and Keh-Yih Su. 2013. Integrating Translation Memory into Phrase-Based Machine Translation during Decoding. In *ACL*.

Wang, Zhiguo, Wael Hamza, and Radu Florian. 2017. Bilateral Multi-perspective Matching for Natural Language Sentences. In *Proceedings of the 26th International Joint Conference on Artificial Intelligence*, IJCAI'17, pages 4144–4150. AAAI Press.

Wuebker, Joern, Patrick Simianer, and John DeNero. 2018. Compact Personalized Models for Neural Machine Translation. In *Proceedings of the 2018 Conference on Empirical Methods in Natural Language Processing*, pages 881–886. Association for Computational Linguistics.

Zhang, Jiajun and Chengqing Zong. 2016. Exploiting Source-side Monolingual Data in Neural Machine Translation. In *Proceedings of the 2016 Conference on Empirical Methods in Natural Language Processing*, pages 1535–1545. Association for Computational Linguistics.

Zhang, Jingyi, Masao Utiyama, Eiichro Sumita, Graham Neubig, and Satoshi Nakamura. 2018. Guiding Neural Machine Translation with Retrieved Translation Pieces. In *Proceedings of the 2018 Conference of the North American Chapter of the Association for Computational Linguistics: Human Language Technologies, Volume 1 (Long Papers)*, pages 1325–1335. Association for Computational Linguistics.

Zoph, Barret, Deniz Yuret, Jonathan May, and Kevin Knight. 2016. Transfer Learning for Low-Resource Neural Machine Translation. In *Proceedings of the 2016 Conference on Empirical Methods in Natural Language Processing*, pages 1568–1575. Association for Computational Linguistics.

Corpus Building for Low Resource Languages in the DARPA LORELEI Program

Jennifer Tracey, Stephanie Strassel, Ann Bies, Zhiyi Song, Michael Arrigo, Kira Griffitt,
Dana Delgado, Dave Graff, Seth Kulick, Justin Mott and Neil Kuster
Linguistic Data Consortium
3600 Market Street, Suite 810
Philadelphia, PA 19104
`{garjen|strassel|bies|zhiyi|marrigo|kiragrif|`
`danafore|graff|kulick|jmott|neilkus@ldc.upenn.edu}`

Abstract

We describe corpora for the LORELEI (Low Resource Languages for Emergent Incidents) Program, whose goal is to build human language technologies to provide situational awareness during emergent incidents, with a particular focus on low resource languages. Incident Language packs are used for system development and testing in machine translation, entity disambiguation and linking, and the "situation frame" task, which requires aggregation of information about the emergent incident. Incident languages, as well as the incidents themselves, remain unknown until the evaluation begins, and no labeled training data is provided; systems developers must rapidly adapt technology for the incident language and return initial results within 24 hours. Given this surprise language evaluation scenario, Representative Language packs are designed to support research into cross-language projection and language universals rather than to provide training data. They contain large volumes of monolingual and parallel text, basic annotations, lexical resources and simple NLP tools for 23 languages selected for typological diversity and coverage. We discuss the creation of the LORELEI language packs with a special focus on resources for machine translation, as well as techniques for maintaining consistency across the language packs.

1 Introduction

The DARPA (Defense Advanced Research Projects Agency) LORELEI Program aims to improve the performance of human language technologies capable of providing situational awareness in the context of a specific natural disaster or other emergent incident, with a particular focus on low resource languages for which existing natural language processing (NLP) technology including machine translation is insufficient to support the use case. Systems are required to process information about topics, entities, relations and sentiment, where both the incident language(s) and the incident type(s) remain unknown until the evaluation starts, and where initial system output is due in just 24 hours.

Specialized data is crucial to achieving these ambitious goals. Linguistic Data Consortium (LDC) has created two types of linguistic resources to support training, development and evaluation of machine translation (MT) and other language technologies for LORELEI: Incident Language (IL) packs and Representative Language (RL) packs. Incident Language packs are designed for LORELEI system development and testing. Systems are evaluated against a human gold standard reference for three tasks: machine translation, entity disambiguation and linking, and "situation frame", which requires aggregation of basic information about the needs and issues resulting from the emergent incident. MT output is also subject to human assessment to gauge its utility for of the situation frame task.

Along with a blind test set, Incident Language packs include a small "rapid adaptation" training set containing the type of found data that might be discoverable for a low resource language at the outset of an incident. We have created Incident Language packs in seven languages to date, with two more currently in progress to support the final LORELEI program evaluation in summer 2019. The IL languages appear in Table 1.

Kinyarwanda	Uyghur
Oromo	Uzbek
Sinhala	IL11 (undisclosed)
Tigrinya	IL12 (undisclosed)
Ukrainian	

Table 1: LORELEI Incident Languages

Representative Language packs contain resources in 20 languages that have been selected to provide broad typological coverage, with languages ranging from higher resourced (Spanish) to very low resourced (Akan). Partial language packs exist for three additional languages. Because evaluation languages remain unknown to system developers until the start of the test period, RL packs are designed to support research into utilization of language universals and projection from related-language resources, rather than serving as training data tailored to particular evaluation tasks in a pre-specified language. Each RL pack contains large volumes of monolingual and parallel text, along with smaller amounts of manual entity annotation and linking, light semantic role labeling, document-level labeling of situational needs and issues, as well as a lexicon and basic tools such as tokenizers and sentence segmenters, plus a grammatical sketch for the language. Some RL packs include supplemental morphological or syntactic resources. Every RL pack also shares a common set of English documents translated into the RL; when this set is combined across all RLs it comprises a 21-way parallel corpus. The RL languages appear in Table 2.

Akan (Twi)	Swahili
Amharic	Tagalog
Arabic	Tamil
Bengali	Thai
Farsi	Vietnamese
Hindi	Wolof
Hungarian	Yoruba
Indonesian	Zulu
Mandarin	English (partial)
Russian	Hausa (partial)
Somali	Turkish (partial)
Spanish	

Table 2: LORELEI Representative Languages

In the sections that follow we discuss the process used to create the LORELEI language packs, with a particular focus on resources to support machine translation research. We also discuss strategies for maintaining compatibility and consistency in data collection, translation and annotation efforts across all LORELEI languages.

2 Monolingual Test, Parallel Text and Lexicons

LORELEI RL and IL language packs contain a number of components specifically designed to support machine translation research, including large volumes of monolingual and parallel or comparable text as well as rich lexical resources.

2.1 Monolingual Text

Both Representative and Incident Language Packs contain large volumes of monolingual text, primarily focusing on data in the LORELEI domain of emergent situations like natural disasters, and spanning a range of genres from formal news to informal social media, blogs and discussion forums to reference materials like Wikipedia. The minimum target for monolingual text in the RLs was 2 million words; actual data yields ranged from over 1.25 billion words on the high end (Russian) to 600,000 words on the low end (Wolof, the only language to fall below the minimum target). IL minimum targets were lower, and final data volumes ranged from 3 million words (Oromo) to 27 million words (Uyghur). Reaching the minimum data volume targets for ILs proved to be a particular challenge, especially for some genres; this was exacerbated by the need for the IL test sets to be primarily comprised of documents about the particular test incident(s). We relied heavily on IL native speakers to use creative search techniques to find test incident data, and often needed to stretch the boundaries of traditional genre definitions to satisfy minimum IL data volume targets.

The data collection process involved seeding the corpus with documents known to be in the LORELEI domain generally (for RLs) or about the particular test incident(s) (for ILs). Native speakers for each language searched the web for suitable sources in their language, selecting particular documents with incident- or domain-relevant topics as well as full websites that contain large volumes of appropriate general content for that language. Incident keywords were also used to identify additional in-domain documents for each language. Each website or document selected for inclusion in the corpus was then harvested using an extension of LDC's web collection infrastructure first developed in the DARPA BOLT Program (Garland et. al. 2012). Harvested text was tokenized and sentence-segmented using LORELEI tools designed for cross-language consistency, supplemented with existing open source tools where necessary, and encoding was standardized to UTF-8. The Google CLD2 language detector was used to filter out harvested text not in the target language. CLD2 performance varied considerably by language and genre; moreover, data for many languages contained some degree of code switching and orthographic variation. Therefore, automatic language ID was intended to locate pervasive problems with a data source, rather than detect every case of non-target text in the corpus. Given this, documents subject to manual translation and annotation received an additional manual audit pass to verify language, content and domain relevance.

All collected sources were also reviewed for Intellectual Property Rights issues prior to distribution, and where necessary language packs include pointers to the original data rather than downloaded/processed data. Language packs include utilities for corpus users to download and process such data, to ensure that they end up with the same versions of the data LDC used throughout our data pipeline.

2.2 Parallel and Comparable Text

Representative Language packs contain a minimum of 1 million words of parallel text: 900,000 words of RL source data translated into English, and a common set of 100,000 words translated from English into every RL. The 900,000 word set was drawn from the monolingual text collection for each language, and was designed to contain roughly equal proportions of data from formal news sources and from informal genres like blogs and social media, though the actual distribution varied by language. The common set of 100,000 English words translated into every RL contained four components: approximately 50% general English news documents, 25% LORELEI-domain English news documents, with the remaining 25% consisting of a phrasebook and elicitation corpus originally developed for the REFLEX (Research on English and Foreign Language Exploitation) Program and subsequently updated for LORELEI (Alvarez et al., 2006). Because the same 100,000-word English set was translated into all 20 RLs, the result is a 21-way parallel corpus spanning a broad range of language families and typologies.

We used three methods to produce parallel text for the Representative Languages: 1) scraping parallel text from the web; 2) obtaining translations through crowdsourcing; and 3) obtaining translations from translation vendors. This combination of methods resulted in translations of varying quality and quantity across languages, but the goal was always the same: to produce sentence-aligned content-accurate translations.

Wherever possible translation targets were met by scraping existing parallel text from the web. In addition to harvesting parallel text sources identified by native speakers, we used BITS (Ma and Liberman, 1999) to locate additional sources of parallel text from the web. BITS scans a list of potential parallel websites, downloads content from those websites and uses translation lexicons constructed for LORELEI to perform language ID on the individual webpages and identify any that are translations of one another. The document pairs are then sentence aligned using Champollion (Ma, 2006), which calculates similarity scores between tokenized segments from both languages to reach the optimal alignment.

When found parallel text was insufficient to meet data volume targets, we turned to crowdsourcing, using two platforms: Amazon Mechanical Turk (https://www.mturk.com/) and CrowdTrans (https://crowdtrans.com/), a platform first developed under LORELEI. Initial crowdsourcing efforts focused on translation of English news sources into RLs, with good yields for Spanish, Russian and Arabic. Subsequent efforts were limited to languages with very large pools of crowd workers, namely Hindi and Benglai, and focused on RL-into-English data. Translation proceeded one segment at a time in order to maintain accurate sentence alignment across languages. Segments resulting in at least 3 crowd translations were also subject to a crowdsourced best-to-worst ranking task for additional quality control. Within the CrowdTrans platform we also used native speaker Community Managers to vet workers before translation to improve the overall quality.

When the combined yield from crowdsourcing and found parallel text did not satisfy the target data volume for a given language, we relied on experienced LDC translation vendors who translated whole documents, maintaining sentence-to-sentence correspondence across the language pairs. Unsurprisingly, we relied most heavily on translation vendors for the lowest-resourced languages, where there was very little existing parallel text on the web and where there were too few workers to make crowdsourcing viable.

Taken together, the LORELEI Representative Language packs provide nearly 42 million words of parallel text, of which 68% came from found data, 5% from crowdsourcing and 27% from translation vendors. Figure 1 shows the relative use of each method across the Representative Languages. Note that for some languages like Chinese and Arabic, existing high quality vendor translations were already available from prior DARPA language programs, so very little new translation was produced using any method.

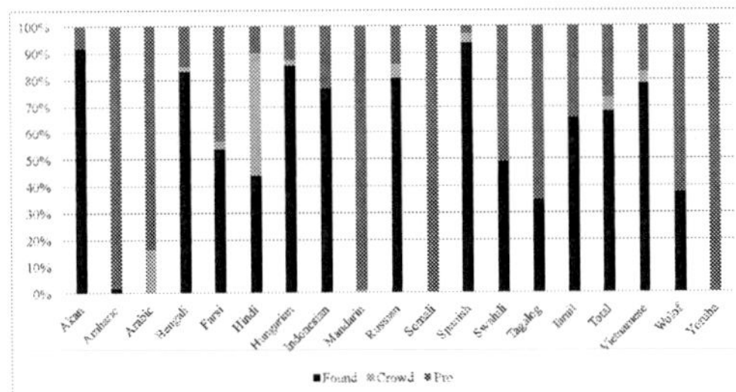

Figure 1: Translation Methods for LORELEI Representative Languages

Incident Language packs include up to 75,000 words of IL data with high quality (one-way, two-way or four-way) manual English translations for system evaluation. They were designed to include an additional 300,000 words of found parallel text for rapid system adaptation into the IL; ideally at least some of this adaptation data is relevant to the evaluation incident or at least relevant to the LORELEI domain. When compared with the Representative Languages, LORELEI ILs are very low resource, and in many cases sufficient volumes of parallel text simply do not exist on the web to satisfy the 300,000 word target. In these cases we provided much larger volumes of comparable text instead. To produce IL comparable text we harvested large volumes of data in both the IL and English, including multilingual data from the same website where possible. We created multilingual clusters following Kutuzov et al. (2016), with document vectors obtained using the method described in Arora et al (2017). The resulting clusters were then augmented by assigning individual Incident Language documents to English-only clusters whose centroid was maximally similar to the IL document. Native speakers reviewed the results to prune, merge and split clusters as needed to improve the overall quality.

2.3 Lexicons

Each Representative Language pack includes a lexicon encompassing an inventory of at least 10,000 headwords/lemmas with part-of-speech, English gloss, and optionally (where appropriate and available) morphological information. The lexicon is comprised of found resources like existing online dictionaries, etc., with some manual effort by native speakers to create new entries as needed to ensure adequate coverage, focusing effort on high frequency tokens missing from the found resources.

For several languages, extensive morphological information is included in a separate word-forms table indexed to the entries in the lexicon. For Arabic, morphological information comes from the Penn Arabic TreeBank (Kulick, et al., 2010); for Amharic, Farsi, Hungarian, Russian, Somali, Spanish and Yoruba, morphological information comes from the Unimorph Project (Kirov, et al., 2018).

For Incident Languages, a custom lexicon is not created, but pointers to available online monolingual and bilingual dictionaries are provided, and where terms of use permit redistribution, the dictionaries are included in the corpus. ILs also include other found grammatical resources like gazetteers, grammars and primers.

3 Annotation Resources

In addition to monolingual and parallel text, LORELEI Language Packs contain several types of manual annotation.

3.1 Entity Annotation

LORELEI Language Packs include three kinds of entity annotation resources: Simple Named Entity, Full Entity, and Entity Linking. In Simple Named Entity (SNE) annotation, text is labeled for names of persons, organizations, locations/ facilities, and geopolitical entities. Full Entity (FE) annotation adds nominal and pronominal mentions of the same types, as well as titles for person entities (such as job titles); it also adds document-level entity coreference. In Entity Linking, named entity mentions are linked to a reference knowledge base developed for LORELEI based on existing external resources. A total of 75,000 words per representative language was labeled for SNE, while an additional 25,000 words was labeled for FE and Entity Linking. Incident Language Pack test sets were also labeled for SNE and EDL.

3.2 Semantic Annotation

Representative Language Packs contain two semantic annotation types developed to support LORELEI research and evaluation: Simple Semantic Annotation (SSA) and Situation Frame (SF). Both SSA and SF label basic information relevant to humanitarian aid and disaster relief scenarios. Situation Frame annotation directly corresponds to the LORELEI SF evaluation task, with a focus on the kind of information that monolingual English-speaking mission planners might require in order to direct a response to an incident as it unfolds. For each document annotators identify the kinds of needs that exist in each location, as well as issues such as civil unrest that might affect the provision of humanitarian assistance, along with the entities involved in the incident. Annotations are at the document level and do not involve extracting specific text extents to justify each Situation Frame. Each annotated frame also includes information about the status, scope, and severity of the needs and issues, as well as sentiment or emotion expressed toward them. SSA represents a more general approach to semantic annotation, labeling basic information about physical events and disaster-relevant situations, their participants, and their locations, with annotations tied to specific text extents in the data. SF appears in both RL and IL packs, while SSA appears only in RL packs.

3.3 Morphosyntactic Annotation

Two types of morphological and syntactic annotation appear in the Representative Language Packs. A 10,000-word subset of the data labeled for both Full Entity and Simple Semantic Annotation is further annotated to identify maximal, non-overlapping Noun Phrases (NPs). Annotators follow surface syntactic structure, applying constituency tests to determine where to mark NPs. After the first 10 RLs were created, a programmatic decision was made to put more annotation effort toward entity and Situation Frame annotation, and so NP annotation was not added to the remaining RLs.

Morphological segmentation was also performed for nine languages; these languages were selected to include a variety of morphological features including robust case marking systems and noun class systems, the use of infixes, circumfixes, reduplication, etc. The nine languages selected were Akan, Hindi, Hungarian, Indonesian, Russian, Spanish, Swahili, Tagalog, and Tamil. For each of these languages, 2000 tokens were segmented at morpheme boundaries, along with markup to indicate substitution (as in *give/gave* in English).

3.4 Parallel Annotation Set

As noted above, all Representative Language packs share a common set of documents translated from English into the RL. From this common set, a smaller 2000-word set was selected for parallel annotation in both the original English and the RL translation. This means that the same translated-from-English document set has been annotated in English and in each of 20 RLs, for all of the following tasks: Simple Named Entity, Full Entity, Entity Linking, Simple Semantic Annotation, and Situation Frame. This data has also been labeled for Noun Phrase Chunking in the 10 RL languages where that task was completed.

4 Grammatical Sketches and Tools

Beyond monolingual text, parallel text and annotations, Representative Language Packs also include grammatical sketches focusing on paradigms and basic grammatical descriptions intended to convey practical information about how to work with the language, rather than deep theoretical discussions or nuanced explication of exceptional cases. Sketches for all languages follow a single template, and include basic information about the language (classification, ISO code, word order, etc.), orthography (characters, variation, word boundaries, etc.), encoding (Unicode chart, etc.), morphology, syntax, and specialized subgrammars for personal names, locations, and numbers, as well as information about variation and references to in-depth grammars. IL packs do not include a customs grammatical sketch, but they do include pointers to grammatical resources about the IL, in the Incident Language and/or in English.

LORELEI RL packs also include basic NLP tools, intended to provide baseline-level performance rather than state-of-the-art. These tools include a transliterator for languages written in non-Roman scripts, tokenizers, sentence segmenters, and named entity taggers. For languages with whitespace-delimited words, we create a custom tokenizer that operates on a series of regular expressions that dictate how to tokenize while preserving web-text artifacts such as hashtags and URLs as single tokens. For languages that do not use whitespace at word boundaries, we rely on existing widely-used tokenizers. Sentence segmentation is performed using an implementation of the Punkt algorithm based on the version found in NLTK (Kiss et. al. 2006). The named entity tagger is a custom conditional random field-based named entity tagger for each RL, trained on the named entity annotations described above.

5 Evaluation Resources for Machine Translation

The primary machine translation evaluation for LORELEI relies on one-way, two-way or four-way gold standard manual translation of an incident-focused test set for each IL. This test data is supplemented by two additional MT evaluation resources: Assessment and HyTER.

5.1 Assessment of MT Output for the Situation Frame Task

Although manual annotation of Situation Frames did not involve selecting a segment of text to justify each frame, LORELEI systems were required to output a single segment that justified both the frame type (e.g. *need for food*) and its place (e.g. *Hela*). These justification segments were subject to manual assessment for both the quality of the MT output and the utility of the selected segment for providing situational awareness within the context of the Situation Frame task. For all cases where the LORELEI system produced a Situation Frame that matched a gold standard reference Situation Frame on the same document, assessors reviewed that frame's justification segment across several dimensions. First, assessors were asked whether the MT for the selected justification segment was sufficiently intelligible to make subsequent assessment decisions, or if additional document context and/or the manual translation was required. The assessor then determined whether the situation frame type was justified by this segment, and if so, whether the place was also justified. If the segment was insufficient to justify either type or place, the assessor was shown the human translation for the segment and asked the same questions. A justification segment like "*People starving in Hela*" would be judged as being sufficiently intelligible and as justifying both the type and the place; while a justification segment like "*Food supply it run short*" would be assessed as intelligible and as justifying need but not place.

5.2 HyTER Annotation

To provide additional resources for diagnostic MT scoring in LORELEI, LDC produced a set of data annotated for HyTER. HyTER (Hybrid Translation Edit Rate) is an annotation approach that results in an exponential number of possible translations for a given sentence, thus producing large reference networks for translation evaluation (Dreyer and Marcu, 2012). We produced HyTER annotation for 645 English gold standard reference translation segments selected from the Uyghur Incident Language test set. One of the four available references was selected as the primary input reference for each segment. For each primary segment we performed two independent HyTER annotation passes, followed by a quality control pass on each segment. This effort yielded nearly 1.2×10^{15} unique meaning equivalents from the original 645 reference segments, with a median of 350,000 meaning equivalents per segment.

6 Maintaining Cross-Language Consistency

The research that underlies LORELEI system development relies in part on cross-lingual transfer approaches, as well as exploitation of language universals. As such, it is important for the RL language packs to be uniform and consistent in their design and implementation. At the same time, the RLs were selected specifically for their typological diversity. To achieve maximum compatibility across language packs while respecting the specific properties of each individual language, we adopted a number of strategies.

At the most basic level, the structure and core components for all language packs are the same, with consistent documentation and file formats across all corpora. All data collection and annotation efforts utilized a central database, enabling consistent handling of the data pipeline. We also used the same tools across all languages for data pre-processing wherever possible. For instance, all whitespace-delimited languages share a single tokenizer, whose rules were intentionally kept simple and were largely punctuation-based in order to increase uniformity across languages. While language-specific extensions to the rule set were possible, they were kept to the bare minimum.

We also used a shared inventory of tagsets and annotation labels across languages. For instance, Part of Speech tags in all RL lexicons are based on the 12 universal POS tags defined in Petrov et al. (2012), and all languages share the same entity and situation frame types and type definitions. Concepts shared across different annotation tasks utilized shared definitions and approaches. For instance, several LORELEI annotation tasks rely on annotators marking the extent of some phenomenon (like a named entity), so rules for selecting extents were defined in a uniform way across tasks and languages. All annotation is token-based rather than character-based; since tokens are defined using shared rules across all languages, this further reducing language-specific variation resulting from low-level annotation decisions.

To further enhance consistency in annotation, we developed template-based language-independent annotation guidelines which were then customized for each of the RL and IL languages as needed. We used the same policies across all languages for how to make decisions in the case of necessary language-specific extensions to the default approach. To achieve this, we first identified key questions about language features that could influence annotation, for instance, whether a language has possessive compound noun construction (e.g. Arabic idafa). Grammatical sketches for every language described whether the language possessed any of these annotation-relevant features, and if so how the phenomenon was realized in that language. The annotation guidelines template then provided a "menu" of options for how to localize the guidelines: if language has feature A, invoke section 3.6; if language has feature B, invoke section 4.8, and so on. This approach ensured consistency across languages within a task since languages with the same features get the same annotation treatment. It also ensured consistency in annotation approaches across tasks. Grammatical sketches themselves also follow the same template for all languages.

Finally, prior to data distribution, all language packs – both Representative and Incident – were subject to independent quality review by an external team including native speaker linguists. Among other factors, the independent QC team reviewed data for conformity to the pre-established language universal annotation policies and template-based guidelines.

7   Conclusion

Taken as a whole, the LORELEI Representative and Incident Language Packs represent a rich new resource for machine translation and natural language technology development in a low resource language setting. The Representative Language packs provide coverage of 23 typologically diverse languages, including some very low resource languages for which existing corpora are scarce. Beyond providing new data for these particular languages, the breadth of data and annotation types and the consistency of data components, corpus creation methods and annotation/translation approaches across the language packs is designed to support new research directions in the use of language universals and cross-language transfer. For MT research in particular the 23-way parallel text corpus represents a valuable new resource. The Incident Language Packs provide carefully curated test sets with gold standard translations and annotations for system development and testing. To date we have distributed representative language packs in 20 languages, as well as partial Representative Language Packs in three additional languages, to LORELEI performers. We have created seven Incident Language Packs; two additional Incident Language Packs are in progress to support the final LORELEI evaluation in 2019. LORELEI Representative and Incident Language Packs for all languages will begin to appear in the LDC Catalog in Fall 2019, making these resources broadly available to the research community at large.

8   Acknowledgements

This material is based upon work supported by the Defense Advanced Research Projects Agency (DARPA) under Contract No. HR0011-15-C-0123. Any opinions, findings and conclusions or recommendations expressed in this material are those of the author(s) and do not necessarily reflect the views of DARPA. The authors gratefully acknowledge Lori Levin, Chris Callison-Burch, Neville Ryant, Jonathan Wright, Brian Gainor, Christopher Caruso, Alex Shelmire, and the hundreds of LORELEI native speaker annotators for their contributions to this research.

References

Alvarez, Alison, Lori Levin, Robert Frederking, Simon Fung, Donna Gates, Jeff Good. 2006. The MILE Corpus for Less Commonly Taught Languages, In *Proceedings of the Human Language Technology Conference of the NAACL, Companion Volume: Short Papers*. Association for Computational Linguistics, pages 5-8.

Arora, Sanjeev, Yingyu Liang, and Tengyu Ma. 2017. A simple but tough to beat baseline for sentence embeddings. 2017. In International Conference on Learning Representations (ICLR 2017)

Compact Language Detector 2. [Online]. Available: https: //code.google.com/p/cld2/

DARPA LORELEI website, retrieved May 24, 2019. https://www.darpa.mil/program/low-resource-languages-for-emergent-incidents

Dreyer, Markus and Daniel Marcu. 2012. HyTER: Meaning-Equivalent Semantics for Translation Evaluation. *Conference of the North American Chapter of the Association for Computational Linguistics: Human Language Technologies*, Montreal, Canada 162–171.

Garland, Jennifer, Stephanie Strassel, Safa Ismael, Zhiyi Song, Haejoong Lee. 2012. Linguistic Resources for Genre-Independent Language Technologies: User-Generated Content in BOLT. *LREC 2012: 8th International Conference on Language Resources and Evaluation*, Istanbul, Turkey.

Kirov, Christo, Ryan Cotterell, John Sylak-Glassman, Géraldine Walther, Ekaterina Vylomova, Patrick Xia, Manaal Faruqui, Sebastian Mielke, Arya D. McCarthy, Sandra Kübler, David Yarowsky, Jason Eisner and Mans Hulden. 2018. UniMorph 2.0: Universal Morphology. *LREC 2018: 11th International Conference on Language Resources and Evaluation*, Miyazaki, Japan

Kiss, Tibor, Jan Strunkt. 2006. Unsupervised multilingual sentence boundary detection. *Computational Linguistics* 32: 455-525.

Kulick, Seth, Ann Bies, Mohamed Maamouri. 2010. Consistent and Flexible Integration of Morphological Annotation in the Arabic Treebank. *LREC 2010: 7th International Conference on Language Resources and Evaluation* Valletta, Malta.

Kutuzov, Andrey, Mikhail Kopotev, Tatyana Sviridenko, Lyubov Ivanova. 2016. Clustering Comparable Corpora of Russian and Ukrainian Academic Texts: Word Embeddings and Semantic Fingerprints. *Proceedings of the Ninth Workshop on Building and Using Comparable Corpora,* Portorož, Slovenia

Ma, Xiaoyi. 2006. Champollion: A Robust Parallel Text Sentence Aligner. *LREC 2006: 5th International Conference on Language Resources and Evaluation*, Genoa, Italy

Ma, Xiaoyi, Mark Liberman. 1999. BITS: A Method for Bilingual Text Search over the Web. *Machine Translation Summit VII:* Singapore, September 13-17

Petrov, Slav, Dipanjan Das, and Ryan McDonald. 2012. A universal part-of-speech tagset. *LREC 2012: 8th International Conference on Language Resources and Evaluation*, Istanbul, Turkey.

Multilingual Multimodal Machine Translation for Dravidian Languages utilizing Phonetic Transcription

Bharathi Raja Chakravarthi,
Bernardo Stearns, Mihael Arcan,
Manel Zarrouk, and John P. McCrae
Insight Centre for Data Analytics
National University of Ireland Galway
Galway, Ireland
`name.surname@insight-centre.org`

Ruba Priyadharshini
Saraswathi Narayanan College,
Madurai, India
Arun Jayapal
Smart Insights from Conversations,
Hyderabad, India
S. Sridevy
Tamil Nadu Agricultural University,
Coimbatore, India

Abstract

Multimodal machine translation is the task of translating from a source text into the target language using information from other modalities. Existing multimodal datasets have been restricted to only highly resourced languages. In addition to that, these datasets were collected by manual translation of English descriptions from the Flickr30K dataset. In this work, we introduce MMDravi, a Multilingual Multimodal dataset for under-resourced Dravidian languages. It comprises of 30,000 sentences which were created utilizing several machine translation outputs. Using data from MMDravi and a phonetic transcription of the corpus, we build an Multilingual Multimodal Neural Machine Translation system (MMNMT) for closely related Dravidian languages to take advantage of multilingual corpus and other modalities. We evaluate our translations generated by the proposed approach with human-annotated evaluation dataset in terms of BLEU, METEOR, and TER metrics. Relying on multilingual corpora, phonetic transcription, and image features, our approach improves the translation quality for the under-resourced languages.

1 Introduction

The development of a Multilingual Multimodal Neural Machine Translation (MMNMT) system requires multilingual parallel corpora and images which are aligned with the parallel sentences for training. The largest existing dataset containing captions, images, and translations for English, German, French and Czech is the WMT shared task Multi30K dataset which is derived from the Flickr30k dataset (Plummer et al., 2015; Plummer et al., 2017). Typically this data is manually created with the help of bilingual annotators (Elliott et al., 2016), however, for many languages, such resources are not available. In those cases, machine translation can be a useful tool for the quick expansion to new languages by producing candidate translation (Dutta Chowdhury et al., 2018). In order to reduce the amount of time, we pose translation as a post-editing task. We automatically translated the English sentences from the WMT corpus using a pre-trained general domain Statistical Machine Translation (SMT) and Neural Machine Translation (NMT).

Multilingual NMT models (Firat et al., 2016) have been shown to increase the translation quality for under-resourced languages. Closely related Dravidian languages such as Tamil (ISO-639-1: ta), Kannada (ISO-639-1: kn), and Malayalam (ISO-639-1: ml) exhibit a large overlap in their vocabulary and strong syntactic and lexical similarities. Dravidian languages are a family of languages spoken primarily in the southern part of India and spread over South Asia and are considered as under-resourced languages. However, the scripts used to write these languages are different and they differ in their morphology. Recently Chakravarthi et al. (2019) have shown that phonetic transcription of a corpus into Latin script improves the multilingual NMT performance for under-resourced Dravidian languages.

In this paper, we propose applying Multilingual Multimodal NMT for translating between closely related Dravidian languages and English. We created multimodal data using SMT and NMT methods, trained on a general domain corpus for under-resourced languages. Combining multilingual and multimodal data along with a phonetic transcription of the corpus improves translation performance for closely related Dravidian languages is shown in the results.

2 Related Work

To capture rich information from multimodal content available on the Web, especially images with descriptions in English was explored in the content of NMT (Specia et al., 2016a) in the WMT shared task. The WMT shared task also provided resources for other popular languages German, Czech and French (Elliott et al., 2017). Most of those data were expensive, for example, English-German corpus was created by Elliott et al. (2016), and cost €23,000 for data collection (€0.06 per word). Such resources are not available for under-resourced languages. Recent work by (Dutta Chowdhury et al., 2018), carried out experiments by utilizing synthetic data for Hindi-English language pair. In contrast, we created MMDravi as a translation post-editing task by utilizing translations of the English sentences associated with images using SMT and NMT trained on general domain data.

The shared task on Multimodal NMT (MNMT) was introduced by Specia et al. (2016b) to generate image descriptions for a target language, given an image and/or a description in the source language. In previous works on MNMT, the researchers utilized visual context by involving both NMT and Image Description Generation (IDG) features that explicitly uses an encoder-decoder (Cho et al., 2014). However, the encoder-decoder architecture encodes the source sentence into a fixed-length vector. To overcome this drawback (Bahdanau et al., 2015) introduced attention mechanism to focus on parts of the source sentence. The work by Calixto and Liu (2017), carried out different experiments to incorporate visual features into NMT by projecting an image feature vector as words into the source sentence, using the image to initialize the encoder hidden state, and using image features to initialize the decoder hidden state. In Calixto et al. (2017), the author incorporated features through a separate encoder and doubly-attentive attention of the decoder to depend on the

image feature. This allowed them to predict the next word and showed that the image feature improved the translation quality. Although all these approaches have demonstrated the possibility of MNMT, they rely on manually collected corpora but under-resourced languages do not have such resources. Our work follows the doubly-attentive model (Calixto et al., 2017) with MMDravi data for the multilingual model by phonetic transcription.

In Ha et al. (2016) and Johnson et al. (2017), the authors have demonstrated that multilingual NMT improves translation quality. For this, they created multilingual NMT without changing the architecture by introducing special tokens at the beginning of the source sentence indicating the source language and target language as shown in Figure 1. We follow this by introducing special tokens in the source sentence to indicate the target language. Phonetic transcription to Latin script and the International Phonetic Alphabet (IPA) was studied by (Chakravarthi et al., 2019) and showed that Latin script outperforms IPA for the Multilingual NMT of Dravidian languages. We propose to combine multilingual, phonetic transcription and multimodal content to improve the translation quality of under-resourced Dravidian languages. Our contribution is to use the closely related languages from the Dravidian language family to exploit the similar syntax and semantic structures by phonetic transcription of the corpora into Latin script along with image feature to improve the translation quality.

3 Background

3.1 Dravidian Languages

Dravidian languages have individual writing scripts and have been assigned a unique block in the Unicode computing industry standard. The similarity of these languages is that they are all written from left to right, consist of sequences of simple or complex characters and follow an alpha-syllabic writing system in which the individual symbols are syllables (Bhanuprasad and Svenson, 2008). The languages also have different sets of vowels and consonants. Vowels and consonants are atomic but when they are combined with each other they form consonant ligatures. Dravidian languages such as Tamil do not represent differences between aspirated and unaspirated stops, while other Dravidian languages such as Kannada and Malayalam have a large number of loan words from Indo-Aryan languages and support a large number of compound characters resulting from the combination of two consonants symbols (Kumar et al., 2015).

3.2 Phonetic Transcription

Phonetic transcription is the use of phonetic symbols such as IPA or non-native script. As the Dravidian languages under study are written in different scripts, they must be converted to some common representation before training the MM-NMT to take advantage of closely related language resources. Phonetic transcription to Latin script and the International Phonetic Alphabet (IPA) was studied by (Chakravarthi et al., 2019) and showed that Latin script outperforms IPA for the Multilingual NMT Dravidian languages. The improvements in translation performance were shown in terms of the BLEU (Papineni et al., 2002) metric. We used the Indic-trans library by Bhat et al. (2015) for phonetic transcription of corpora into the Latin script, which brings all the languages into a single representation by a phoneme matching algorithm. The same library was used to back-transliterate from Latin script to the corresponding Dravidian language to evaluate the translation performance.

3.3 Neural Machine Translation

Neural Machine Translation is a sequence-to-sequence approach (Sutskever et al., 2014) using an encoder-decoder architecture with an attention mechanism (Bahdanau et al., 2015). Given a source sentence $X = x_1, x_2, x_3, ... x_n$ and target sentence $Y = y_1, y_2, y_3, ... y_n$ the bidirectional encoder transforms the source sentence into annotation vectors $C = h_1, h_2, h_3, ... h_n$. At each time step t, the source context vector c_t is computed based on the annotation vector and the decoder's previous hidden state s_{t-1}. The decoder generates one target word at a time by computing the probability of $P(y_t = k | y_{<t}, c_t)$ given a hidden state s_t as follows

$$P(y_t = k | y_{<t}, c_t)$$
$$\propto \exp(L_0 tanh(L_s s_t +$$
$$L_w E_y[y_{t-1}] + L_c c_t)) \quad (1)$$

The L_0, L_s, L_W and L_c are transformation matrices.

The attention model calculates c_t as the weighted sum of the source side context vectors:

$$c_t = \sum_{i=1}^{N} \alpha_{t,i}^{src} h_i \quad (2)$$

$$\alpha_{t,i}^{src} = \frac{\exp\left(e_{t,i}^{src}\right)}{\sum_{j=1}^{N} \exp\left(e_{t,j}^{src}\right)} \quad (3)$$

$\alpha_{t,i}^{src}$ is the normalized alignment matrix between each source annotation vector h_i and word y_t to be emitted at a time step t. Expected alignment $e_{t,i}^{src}$ between each source annotation vector h_i and the target word y_t is computed using the following formula:

$$e_{t,i}^{src} = (V_a^{src})^T tanh(U_a^{src} s_t' + W_a^{src} h_i) \quad (4)$$

V_a^{src}, U_a^{src} and W_a^{src} are model parameters.

3.4 Multimodal Neural Machine Translation

The Multimodal NMT (MNMT) (Calixto et al., 2017) model is an extension of the encoder-decoder framework, by incorporating visual information. To incorporate the visual features extracted from the pre-trained model the authors have integrated another attention mechanism to the decoder. The doubly-attentive decoder Recurrent Neural Network is conditioned on the previous hidden state, previously emitted word, source sentence and the image via attention mechanism (Calixto et al., 2017). In the original attention-based NMT model described in Section 3.3, a single encoder for the source sentence, a single decoder for the target sentence and the attention mechanism are conditioned on the source sentence. MNMT integrates two separate attention mechanism over the source language and visual features associated with the source and target sentence. The decoder generates a target word by computing a new probability $P(y_t = k | y_{<t}, C, A)$ given a hidden state s_t, the previously emitted word $y_{<t}$, and the two context vectors c_t from encoder of source sentence and i_t from image features.

$$P(y_t = k | y_{<t}, C, A)$$
$$\propto \exp(L_0 tanh(L_s s_t +$$
$$L_w E_y[y_{t-1}] + L_{cs} c_t + L_{ci} i_t)) \quad (5)$$

L_0, L_s, L_w, E_y, L_{cs}, and L_{ci} are projection matrices. The mechanism in MNMT is similar to NMT

Source	__opt_src__en __opt_src__kn a group of people standing in front of an igloo .
Target (ISO-639-1: kn)	ಇಗ್ಲೂ ಮುಂದೆ ನಿಂತಿರುವ ಜನರ ಗುಂಪು.
Source	__opt_src__en __opt_src__ta a group of people standing in front of an igloo .
Target (ISO-639-1: ta)	ஒரு குடில் முன் நின்று மக்கள் குழு.
Source	__opt_src__en __opt_src__ml a group of people standing in front of an igloo .
Target (ISO-639-1: ml)	ഇഗ്ലൂ മുന്നിൽ നിൽക്കുന്ന ഒരു കൂട്ടം ആളുകൾ.

Figure 1: Example of sentences with special tokens to indicate the source and target languages.

with an attention model, except for the source sentence and previous hidden state, it also takes the context vector a from the image features using a double attention layer to calculate the current hidden state. The doubly-attentive model calculates the time-dependent vector i_t as follows:

$$i_t = \beta_t \sum_{l=1}^{L} \alpha_{t,l}^{img} a_l \qquad (6)$$

Where,

$$\beta_t = \sigma(W_\beta s_{t-1} + b_\beta) \qquad (7)$$

The expected alignment vector of image is given by

$$\alpha_{t,l}^{img} = \frac{\exp\left(e_{t,l}^{img}\right)}{\sum_{j=1}^{L} \exp\left(e_{t,j}^{img}\right)} \qquad (8)$$

$$e_{t,l}^{img} = (V_a^{img})^T tanh(U_a^{img} s_t' + W_a^{img} a_l) \qquad (9)$$

V_a^{img}, U_a^{img} and W_a^{img} are model parameters.

	Corpus Statistics		
Lang pair	*sent*	*s-tokens*	*t-tokens*
En-Ta	0.8M	6.4M	13.3M
En-Kn	0.5M	2.6M	4.5M
En-Ml	1.4M	16.7M	23.5M

Table 1: Statistics of the parallel corpora used to train the general domain translation systems. sent: Number of sentences, s-tokens: Number of source tokens, and t-tokens: Number of target tokens.

4 Experimental Setup

4.1 Data

The images required for our work were collected from Flicker by Plummer et al. (2015). The

	BLEU Score	
Lang pair	*SMT*	*NMT*
En-Ta	30.29	35.52
En-Kn	28.81	26.86
En-Ml	36.73	38.56

Table 2: Results of general domain SMT and NMT translation systems on general domain evaluation set

Multi30K dataset contains parallel corpora for English and German. There were two types of multilingual annotations released by Multi30K dataset (Elliott et al., 2016). The first one is an English description for each image and its German translation. The second is a corpus of five independently collected English and German description pairs for each image. Synthetic data or back-transliterated data have been widely used to improve the performance of NMT and MNMT. To produce a target side description of an image, we create a general domain SMT and NMT for English-Tamil, English-Kannada, and English-Malayalam pairs. We collected the general domain parallel corpora for the Dravidian languages from the OPUS website (Tiedemann and Nygaard, 2004) and (Chakravarthi et al., 2018). The corpus statistics are shown in Table 1. The corpus is tokenized and standardized to lowercase. The general domain SMT was created with Moses (Koehn et al., 2007) while the NMT system was trained with OpenNMT (Klein et al., 2017). After tokenization, we fed the parallel corpora to Moses and OpenNMT. Preprocessed files are then used to train the models. We used the default OpenNMT parameters for training, i.e. 2 layers LSTM with 500 hidden units for both, the encoder and decoder.

The SMT and NMT system results on general

Figure 2: Example of sentence and image with candidate translation to choose.

domain evaluation set are shown in Table 2. The development and test set of the multimodal corpus was collected with the help of volunteer annotators. To reduce the annotation time, we posed the translation task of the development and test set as a post-editing task. We provided the candidate translation of the English sentence from SMT, NMT, and an option to choose the best translation or provide an original translation. Eighteen annotators participated in this annotation process, with different backgrounds, they all are native speakers of the language that they annotated. The data for the Malayalam language was collected from three different native speakers. Ten Tamil native speakers participated in creating data for the Tamil language and five Kannada native speakers annotated for the Kannada language. Since voluntary annotators are scarce and annotate little data, each sentence was annotated by only one annotator. We then selected the system that performed better based on the choice of annotators. We designed an annotation tool to meet the objective of method. We decided to use Google Forms to collect the data from the voluntary annotator's. An example is shown in Figure 2. We chose NMT and used the general domain NMT to post-edit the translation for the training set of MMDravi.

For our tasks, all descriptions in English were converted to lowercase and tokenized, while we

Table 3: Results are expressed in BLEU score: Baseline is Multimodal NMT, MMNMT is trained on native script, and MMNMT-T is trained utilizing phonetic transcription.

Lang pair	BLEUscore		
	Baseline	*MMNMT*	*MMNMT-T*
En-Ta	50.2	51.0	**52.3**
En-Ml	35.6	36.0	**36.5**
En-Kn	44.5	45.1	**45.9**
Ta-En	45.2	47.4	**48.9**
Ml-En	34.3	36.2	**37.6**
Kn-En	50.0	50.2	**50.8**

did not have to bother about the case correction for Dravidian languages (as they do not have cases). We tokenized the Dravidian language using the OpenNMT tokenizer with *segment alphabet* options for Tamil, Kannada, and Malayalam. For the sub-word level representation, we chose the 10,000 most frequent units to train the BPE (Sennrich et al., 2016) model. We used this model for the sub-word level segmentation for the training, development, and evaluation set. We trained the MMNMT model to translate from English into Dravidian languages as well as from Dravidian languages into English. Visual features were extracted from publicly available pre-trained CNN's. Specifically, we extract spatial image features using the VGG-19 network (Simonyan and Zisserman, 2014). In our experiment, we pass all the images in our dataset through the pre-trained VGG-19 layered network to extract global information and use them in a separate visual attention mechanism as described in Calixto et al. (2017).

4.2 Multilingual Multimodal Neural Machine Translation

Since we translate between closely related languages and English, we set up the translation setting in two scenarios, 1) One-to-Many and 2) Many-to-One.

4.2.1 One-to-Many Approach

In this setting, we create a model to translate from English into Tamil, Malayalam, and Kannada. The source language sentence was replicated three times for the three languages with a token indicating target language. Figure 1 shows the example of sentences.

src	a black dog runs on green grass with a toy in his mouth .
ref	ஒரு கருப்பு நாய் வாயில் ஒரு பொம்மையுடன் பச்சை புல்லில் ஓடுகிறது.
MMNMT	ஒரு கருப்பு நாய் வாயில் ஒரு பொம்மையுடன் பச்சை புல் மீது இய ங்கும் .
MMNMT -T	ஒரு கருப்பு நாய் வாயில் ஒரு பொம்மையுடன் பச்சை புல் மீது ஓடுகிறத.

Figure 3: Example showing improvement of translation quality and readability of the translation over baseline model. Errors are shown in red color.

src	a woman and two men , that are dressed professionally, are having a discussion.
ref	ஒரு பெண் மற்றும் இரண்டு ஆண்கள், தொழில்முறை உடையணிந்து, ஒரு விவாதத்தில் உள்ளார்கள்.
MMNMT	ஒரு பெண் , மற்றும் இரு ஆண்கள் professionally ஆயத்தம்பண்ணி . ஒரு விவாதத்திலை வேண்டினோம் .
MMNMT -T	ஒரு பெண் மற்றும் இரண்டு ஆண்கள், professional உடையணிந்து, ஒரு விவாதத்தில் உள்ளார.

Figure 4: Example showing translation with accurate transfer of important information. Errors are shown in red color.

4.2.2 Many-to-One Approach

In the many-to-one MMNMT system, we create a model to translate from Tamil, Malayalam, and Kannada (Dravidian languages) to English. We replicated the English sentence three times for three languages on the target side of the corpus. We then train the MNMT system with a visual feature for individual language level with the MM-Dravi data. We compared the results with the MM-NMT for one-to-many and many-to-one models.

4.3 Results

We applied the baseline bilingual Multimodal NMT systems with respect to the MMDravi data created from the Multi30k dataset. Then we trained our MMNMT and MMNMT-T (phonetic transcription of corpus) for English into Dravidian languages and vice versa. Results are presented in BLEU (Papineni et al., 2002) (BiLingual Evaluation Understudy), which measures the n-gram precision with respect to the evaluation set.

Table 3 provides the BLUE scores for the MM-NMT model. We observed that the translation performance of MMNMT is higher compared to the Bilingual Multimodal NMT model in BLEU. Translation from Dravidian to English has the highest improvement in terms of BLEU Score. Our experiments show that the MMNMT system compared with the bilingual system has an improvement in several language directions, which are likely gained from phonetic transcription, image features, and transfer of parameters from different languages.

The results show that for MMNMT with phonetically transcribed corpora, helps more in Dravidian to English than English to Dravidian. An explanation for this is that in the dataset, each source sentence has three targets, which encourages the language model to improve the translation results. In Table 3, we compare the BLEU scores with a baseline approach and our method. In order to evaluate the effectiveness of our proposed model, we have explored MMNMT trained on original scripts and MMNMT trained on a single script. Our empirical results show that the best result is achieved when we phonetically transcribed the corpus and brought it to a single script for both English to Dravidian and Dravidian to English translation tasks.

Figure 3 shows the examples of where the MM-NMT model improves the translation quality and readability of the translation over the baseline model. The results given by the human evaluation confirm the results observed in evaluation BLEU metric. The second example for English-Tamil translation of MMNMT system outperforming the baseline is shown in Figure 4. The first example showns an almost perfect translation obtained with the MMNMT system for English to Tamil. In the second example, translation obtained with the MMNMT system is acceptable with the accurate transfer of important information (Coughlin, 2003). This suggests the synthetic data with our MMNMT model can be used in an under-resourced language setting to improve the translation quality.

5 Conclusion

We introduced a new dataset, named MMDravi and proposed a MMNMT method for closely related Dravidian languages to overcome the resource issues. Compared to the baseline approach, the results show that our approach can improve translation quality, especially for Dravidian languages. Our evaluation, using phonetic transcription, multilingual and multimodal NMT, has shown that the proposed MMNMT-T outperforms the existing approach of multimodal, multilingual in low-resource neural machine translation across all the language pairs considered. We plan to release multilingual translations as an addition to Flickr30k set, and explore the effect of the quality of this synthetic data in our future work.

Acknowledgments

This work is supported by a research grant from Science Foundation Ireland, co-funded by the European Regional Development Fund, for the Insight Centre under Grant Number SFI/12/RC/2289 and the European Union's Horizon 2020 research and innovation programme under grant agreement No 731015, ELEXIS - European Lexical Infrastructure and grant agreement No 825182, Prêt-à-LLOD.

References

Bahdanau, Dzmitry, Kyunghyun Cho, and Yoshua Bengio. 2015. Neural machine translation by jointly learning to align and translate. In *3rd International Conference on Learning Representations, ICLR 2015, San Diego, CA, USA, May 7-9, 2015, Conference Track Proceedings*.

Bhanuprasad, Kamadev and Mats Svenson. 2008. Errgrams – a way to improving ASR for highly inflected Dravidian languages. In *Proceedings of the Third International Joint Conference on Natural Language Processing: Volume-II*.

Bhat, Irshad Ahmad, Vandan Mujadia, Aniruddha Tammewar, Riyaz Ahmad Bhat, and Manish Shrivastava. 2015. IIIT-H System Submission for FIRE2014 Shared Task on Transliterated Search. In *Proceedings of the Forum for Information Retrieval Evaluation*, FIRE '14, pages 48–53, New York, NY, USA. ACM.

Calixto, Iacer and Qun Liu. 2017. Incorporating global visual features into attention-based neural machine translation. In *Proceedings of the 2017 Conference on Empirical Methods in Natural Language Processing*, pages 992–1003. Association for Computational Linguistics.

Calixto, Iacer, Qun Liu, and Nick Campbell. 2017. Doubly-attentive decoder for multi-modal neural machine translation. In *Proceedings of the 55th Annual Meeting of the Association for Computational Linguistics (Volume 1: Long Papers)*, pages 1913–1924. Association for Computational Linguistics.

Chakravarthi, Bharathi Raja, Mihael Arcan, and John P. McCrae. 2018. Improving Wordnets for Under-Resourced Languages Using Machine Translation. In *Proceedings of the 9th Global WordNet Conference*. The Global WordNet Conference 2018 Committee.

Chakravarthi, Bharathi Raja, Mihael Arcan, and John P. McCrae. 2019. Comparison of Different Orthographies for Machine Translation of Under-resourced Dravidian Languages. In *Proceedings of the 2nd Conference on Language, Data and Knowledge*.

Cho, Kyunghyun, Bart van Merrienboer, Caglar Gulcehre, Dzmitry Bahdanau, Fethi Bougares, Holger Schwenk, and Yoshua Bengio. 2014. Learning phrase representations using RNN encoder–decoder for statistical machine translation. In *Proceedings of the 2014 Conference on Empirical Methods in Natural Language Processing (EMNLP)*, pages 1724–1734, Doha, Qatar, October. Association for Computational Linguistics.

Coughlin, Deborah. 2003. Correlating automated and human assessments of machine translation quality. In *In Proceedings of MT Summit IX*, pages 63–70.

Dutta Chowdhury, Koel, Mohammed Hasanuzzaman, and Qun Liu. 2018. Multimodal neural machine translation for low-resource language pairs using synthetic data. In *Proceedings of the Workshop on Deep Learning Approaches for Low-Resource NLP*, pages 33–42, Melbourne, July. Association for Computational Linguistics.

Elliott, Desmond, Stella Frank, Khalil Sima'an, and Lucia Specia. 2016. Multi30K: Multilingual English-German Image Descriptions. In *Proceedings of the 5th Workshop on Vision and Language*, pages 70–74. Association for Computational Linguistics.

Elliott, Desmond, Stella Frank, Loïc Barrault, Fethi Bougares, and Lucia Specia. 2017. Findings of the Second Shared Task on Multimodal Machine Translation and Multilingual Image Description. In *Proceedings of the Second Conference on Machine Translation*, pages 215–233. Association for Computational Linguistics.

Firat, Orhan, Kyunghyun Cho, and Yoshua Bengio. 2016. Multi-way, multilingual neural machine translation with a shared attention mechanism. In *Proceedings of the 2016 Conference of the North American Chapter of the Association for Computational Linguistics: Human Language Technologies*, pages 866–875. Association for Computational Linguistics.

Ha, Thanh-Le, Jan Niehues, and Alexander H. Waibel. 2016. Toward multilingual neural machine translation with universal encoder and decoder. *CoRR*, abs/1611.04798.

Johnson, Melvin, Mike Schuster, Quoc V. Le, Maxim Krikun, Yonghui Wu, Zhifeng Chen, Nikhil Thorat, Fernanda Viégas, Martin Wattenberg, Greg Corrado, Macduff Hughes, and Jeffrey Dean. 2017. Google's multilingual neural machine translation system: Enabling zero-shot translation. *Transactions of the Association for Computational Linguistics*, 5:339–351, December.

Klein, Guillaume, Yoon Kim, Yuntian Deng, Jean Senellart, and Alexander Rush. 2017. OpenNMT: Open-Source Toolkit for Neural Machine Translation. In *Proceedings of ACL 2017, System Demonstrations*, pages 67–72. Association for Computational Linguistics.

Koehn, Philipp, Hieu Hoang, Alexandra Birch, Chris Callison-Burch, Marcello Federico, Nicola Bertoldi, Brooke Cowan, Wade Shen, Christine Moran, Richard Zens, Chris Dyer, Ondrej Bojar, Alexandra Constantin, and Evan Herbst. 2007. Moses: Open Source Toolkit for Statistical Machine Translation. In *Proceedings of the 45th Annual Meeting of the Association for Computational Linguistics Companion Volume Proceedings of the Demo and Poster Sessions*, pages 177–180. Association for Computational Linguistics.

Kumar, Arun, Lluís Padró, and Antoni Oliver. 2015. Joint Bayesian morphology learning for Dravidian languages. In *Proceedings of the Joint Workshop on Language Technology for Closely Related Languages, Varieties and Dialects*, pages 17–23, Hissar, Bulgaria, September. Association for Computational Linguistics.

Papineni, Kishore, Salim Roukos, Todd Ward, and Wei-Jing Zhu. 2002. BLEU: a Method for Automatic Evaluation of Machine Translation. In *Proceedings of the 40th Annual Meeting of the Association for Computational Linguistics*.

Plummer, Bryan A., Liwei Wang, Chris M. Cervantes, Juan C. Caicedo, Julia Hockenmaier, and Svetlana Lazebnik. 2015. Flickr30k entities: Collecting region-to-phrase correspondences for richer image-to-sentence models. In *Proceedings of the 2015 IEEE International Conference on Computer Vision (ICCV)*, ICCV '15, pages 2641–2649, Washington, DC, USA. IEEE Computer Society.

Plummer, Bryan A., Liwei Wang, Chris M. Cervantes, Juan C. Caicedo, Julia Hockenmaier, and Svetlana Lazebnik. 2017. Flickr30k entities: Collecting region-to-phrase correspondences for richer image-to-sentence models. *Int. J. Comput. Vision*, 123(1):74–93, May.

Sennrich, Rico, Barry Haddow, and Alexandra Birch. 2016. Neural Machine Translation of Rare Words with Subword Units. In *Proceedings of the 54th Annual Meeting of the Association for Computational Linguistics (Volume 1: Long Papers)*, pages 1715–1725. Association for Computational Linguistics.

Simonyan, Karen and Andrew Zisserman. 2014. Very deep convolutional networks for large-scale image recognition. *CoRR*, abs/1409.1556.

Specia, Lucia, Stella Frank, Khalil Sima'an, and Desmond Elliott. 2016a. A Shared Task on Multimodal Machine Translation and Crosslingual Image Description. In *Proceedings of the First Conference on Machine Translation: Volume 2, Shared Task Papers*, pages 543–553. Association for Computational Linguistics.

Specia, Lucia, Stella Frank, Khalil Sima'an, and Desmond Elliott. 2016b. A shared task on multimodal machine translation and crosslingual image description. In *Proceedings of the First Conference on Machine Translation*, pages 543–553, Berlin, Germany, August. Association for Computational Linguistics.

Sutskever, Ilya, Oriol Vinyals, and Quoc V. Le. 2014. Sequence to sequence learning with neural networks. In *Proceedings of the 27th International Conference on Neural Information Processing Systems - Volume 2*, NIPS'14, pages 3104–3112, Cambridge, MA, USA. MIT Press.

Tiedemann, Jörg and Lars Nygaard. 2004. The OPUS Corpus - Parallel and Free: http://logos.uio.no/opus. In *Proceedings of the Fourth International Conference on Language Resources and Evaluation (LREC'04)*. European Language Resources Association (ELRA).

A3-108 Machine Translation System for LoResMT 2019

Saumitra Yadav   **Vandan Mujadia**   **Manish Shrivastava**

Machine Translation - Natural Lanugae Processing Lab
Language Technologies Research Centre
Kohli Center on Intelligent Systems
International Institute of Information Technology - Hyderabad
`saumitra.yadav,vandan.mu{@research.iiit.ac.in}`
`m.shrivastava@iiit.ac.in`

Abstract

In this paper, we describe our machine translation systems submitted to LoResMT 2019 Shared Task. Systems were developed for Bhojpuri, Magahi, Sindhi, Latvian $\Longleftrightarrow$ (English). This paper outlines preprocessing , configuration of the submitted systems and the results produced using the same.

1   Introduction

The task of Machine Translation aims to obtain valid translation of text of one language to another. Data driven MT system uses parallel sentences (i.e, x^{th} sentences in two languages show same meaning). For the data driven system to learn translation, it requires sufficient amount of parallel text (bi-text) (Turchi et al., 2008), which is not always easy to get. Scarcity of parallel text can hinder data driven systems ability to give decent translations (Koehn and Knowles, 2017).

For languages like Bhojpuri, Sindhi and Maghai which are primarily spoken in northern India by around 50 million, 1.6 million, 12 million people respectively[1] resources are scarce to obtain a decent machine translation system. As for Latvian, which is spoken by roughly 1.75 million people primarily in Latvia and is one of the official languages of the EU[2]. In LoResMT 2019, we participated as team A3-108 and trained 24 systems for English to (Bhojpuri, Magahi, Sindhi, Latvian) and vice-versa with 3 systems for each direction.

[1] http://www.censusindia.gov.in/2011Census/Language-2011/Statement-1.pdf

[2] https://www.ethnologue.com/18/language/lav/

2   Data

Parallel and monolingual corpora for Bhojpuri, Magahi and Sindhi received for the shared task. Monolingual data for English and Latvian were taken from Goldhahn et al (2012). We included training data to the monolingual corpus of each language for decent language model. Statistics of parallel and monolingual text are presented in Table 1 and 2 respectively.

Language Pair	Train	Dev	Test
eng-bho	28999	500	250
eng-mag	3710	500	250
eng-sin	29014	500	250
eng-lav	54000	1000	500

Table 1: English-low resources languages (eng-English, bho-Bhojpuri, mag-Magahi, sin-Sindhi and lav-Latvian corpus) split statistics. Number indicates number of parallel sentences.

Language	# of sentences
bho	78999
mag	19027
sin	102345
lav	2053998
eng	2410767

Table 2: We concatenate training data with monolingual data for (eng-English, bho-Bhojpuri, mag-Magahi, sin-Sindhi and lav-Latvian corpus).

3   System Description

We utilize both Statistical Machine Translation (SMT) and Neural Machine Translation (NMT) with attention for our systems. Following subsections describe steps involving preprocessing and training configurations for NMT and SMT.

3.1 Preprocessing

Following are the preprocessing steps for both SMT and NMT.

- **Tokenization**: We use IndicNLP Toolkit[3] to tokenize Bhojpuri, Maghai and Sindhi (train, dev, test and monolingual) as a first step. For English and Latvian, we utilize default Moses toolkit[4](Koehn et al., 2007) tokenizer to obtain clean tokenized text.

- Also, for English, we keep letter case as it is to capture syntactic importance e.g. *The* is at start of sentence would roughly be the determinant of subject unlike *the* in the middle of a sentence and to help translate Named entity.

3.2 Training configuration for Neural Machine Translation

NMT make use of neural networks to learn to generate most likely text sequence as output given input text sequence(Sutskever et al., 2014; Bahdanau et al., 2014). Recent work in machine translation make use of self attention(Vaswani et al., 2017) to achieve State of Art results for resource rich language pairs. Due to low resource settings (Koehn and Knowles, 2017), we avoid the use of transformer and explore sequence to sequence with attention architecture (Bahdanau et al., 2014) for our NMT based systems. We make use of Nematus toolkit[5](Sennrich et al., 2017) to carry out our NN based experiments for all 8 directions (English ⟺ Bhojpuri, English ⟺ Magahi, English ⟺ Sindhi and English ⟺ Latvian).

In Table 3, Columns show total number of unique words with minimum count (mc) 2 and 1 in training text for respective language pairs (L1-L2). One can observe that there is a significant increase in unique count between mc>=2 and mc>=1. Hence, vocabulary size increases significantly which affects learning due in low resource settings (because almost half of the vocab has frequency 1). Therefore, we explore Byte Pair Encoding (BPE) (Sennrich et al., 2015) to handle rare words effectively.

Following are hyper-parameters we use in our NMT systems and rest were default as mentioned in Nematus,

- BPE Merge Operations: 5000

- Hidden Layer Dimension of LSTM: 200

- Loss: cross entropy

- Optimizer: Adam

- Beam Size (During Training): 4

- Beam Size (During Testing): 10

- Size of Embedding Layer for **Method1-a**: 50

- Size of Embedding Layer for **Method2-a**: 200

Also, we train two systems in each direction English<>(Bhojpuri, Magahi, Sindhi, Latvian) by keeping dimension of embedding layer to 50 and 200 respectively. We use Adam Optimizer(Kingma and Ba, 2014) with cross entropy loss across all systems.

Language Pair L1 - L2	# of unique words			
	mc>=2		mc >=1	
	L1	L2	L1	L2
eng-bho	6710	8790	12684	19754
eng-mag	2946	3355	5650	6504
eng-sin	6726	7651	12127	15689
eng-lav	16145	32248	27896	60376

Table 3: Number of Unique words in training data for language pairs (eng-English, bho-Bhojpuri, mag-Magahi, sin-Sindhi and lav-Latvian), with minimum count (mc) >=2 and >=1 .

3.3 Training configuration for Statistical Machine Translation

Phrase Based Statistical Machine Translation (PBSMT) is a statistical approach which uses co-occurrence of word sequences across parallel text to learn translation probabilities. SMT utilizes aforementioned probabilities and language model to generate translation text given an input text (Koehn et al., 2003). We make use of Moses toolkit (Koehn et al., 2007) for this paradigm. We also use GIZA++ (Och and Ney, 2003) to find alignments between parallel text and grow-diag-final-and method (Koehn et al., 2003) to extract aligned phrases. We utilize KenLM (Kenneth Heafield, 2011) to train a trigram model with kneser ney smoothing on monolingual corpus of all languages and MERT (Och, 2003) is used for tuning the trained models (named as **Method3-b** in results).

---

[3] http://anoopkunchukuttan.github.io/indic_nlp_library/
[4] https://github.com/mosessmt/mosesdecoder
[5] https://github.com/EdinburghNLP/nematus

Experiment	BLEU	Precision	Recall	F-Measure
Bho2Eng-Method1-a	10.12	16.27	15.46	15.85
Bho2Eng-Method2-a	12.09	18.72	17.67	18.18
Bho2Eng-Method3-b	**17.03**	**22.28**	**22.43**	**22.35**
Eng2Bho-Method1-a	6.19	12.52	11.59	12.04
Eng2Bho-Method2-a	10.5	**18.11**	15.34	16.61
Eng2Bho-Method3-b	**10.69**	16.74	**17.07**	**16.9**
Eng2Lav-Method1-a	17.06	26.74	21.05	23.56
Eng2Lav-Method2-a	28.46	33.71	32.19	32.93
Eng2Lav-Method3-b	**33.78**	**37.75**	**38.55**	**38.15**
Eng2Mag-Method1-a	1.63	8.66	5.95	7.05
Eng2Mag-Method2-a	1.83	9.13	5.09	6.54
Eng2Mag-Method3-b	**9.37**	**16.21**	**17.06**	**16.62**
Eng2Sin-Method1-a	17.43	22.2	22.91	22.55
Eng2Sin-Method2-a	25.17	30.09	29.09	29.58
Eng2Sin-Method3-b	**37.58**	**40.4**	**40.52**	**40.46**
Lav2Eng-Method1-a	31.79	38.45	35.11	36.7
Lav2Eng-Method2-a	37.27	42.68	40.42	41.52
Lav2Eng-Method3-b	**43.6**	**46.86**	**47.59**	**47.22**
Mag2Eng-Method1-a	1.86	8.58	6.37	7.31
Mag2Eng-Method2-a	3.03	10.28	6.67	8.09
Mag2Eng-Method3-b	**9.71**	**16.55**	**17.15**	**16.84**
Sin2Eng-Method1-a	19.11	25.54	24.01	24.75
Sin2Eng-Method2-a	26.68	32.38	30.81	31.58
Sin2Eng-Method3-b	**31.32**	**36.06**	**35.86**	**35.96**

Table 4: Performace of translation systems in terms of BLEU score, Precision, Recall and F-Measure

4 Result

Table 4 shows performance of 24 systems in terms of BLEU (Papineni et al., 2002) score, Precision, Recall and F-Measure. First column (*Experiment field*) shows the language direction and method used. From the table 4, we can see that for each language direction we report three different experiments(1,2 for NMT and 3 for SMT) as described in Section-3.

From the experiments, We observe that SMT is consistently outperforming NMT in low resource settings (Table 4).

- hyperparameters of network along with mention of method 1 and 2

- mention of method 3 in smt

References

Bahdanau, Dzmitry and Cho, Kyunghyun and Bengio, Yoshua 2014. *Neural machine translation by jointly learning to align and translate*, arXiv preprint arXiv:1409.0473

Goldhahn, Dirk and Eckart, Thomas and Quasthoff, Uwe. 2012. *Building Large Monolingual Dictionaries at the Leipzig Corpora Collection: From 100 to 200 Languages.* LREC. Volume 29. 31–43

Heafield, Kenneth 2011. *KenLM: Faster and smaller language model queries*, Proceedings of the sixth workshop on statistical machine translation 187–197 Association for Computational Linguistics

Kingma, Diederik P and Ba, Jimmy 2014. *Adam: A method for stochastic optimization*, arXiv preprint arXiv:1412.6980

Koehn, Philipp and Hoang, Hieu and Birch, Alexandra and Callison-Burch, Chris and Federico, Marcello and Bertoldi, Nicola and Cowan, Brooke and Shen, Wade and Moran, Christine and Zens, Richard and others 2007. *Moses: Open source toolkit for statistical machine translation*, Proceedings of the 45th annual meeting of the association for computational linguistics companion volume proceedings of the demo and poster sessions 177–180

Koehn, Philipp and Och, Franz Josef and Marcu, Daniel 2003. *Statistical phrase-based translation*, Proceedings of the 2003 Conference of the North American Chapter of the Association for Computational Linguistics on Human Language Technology-Volume 1 48–54 Association for Computational Linguistics

Koehn, Philipp and Knowles, Rebecca 2017. *Six challenges for neural machine translation*, arXiv preprint arXiv:1706.03872

Och, Franz Josef and Ney, Hermann 2003. *A Systematic Comparison of Various Statistical Alignment Models*, Computational Linguistics Number 1, Volume 29 19–51

Och, Franz Josef 2003. *Minimum error rate training in statistical machine translation*, Proceedings of the 41st Annual Meeting on Association for Computational Linguistics-Volume 1 160–167 Association for Computational Linguistics

Papineni, Kishore and Roukos, Salim and Ward, Todd and Zhu, Wei-Jing 2002. *BLEU: a method for automatic evaluation of machine translation*, Proceedings of the 40th annual meeting on association for computational linguistics 311–318 Association for Computational Linguistics

Sennrich, Rico and Haddow, Barry and Birch, Alexandra 2015. *Neural machine translation of rare words with subword units*, arXiv preprint arXiv:1508.07909

Sennrich, Rico and Firat, Orhan and Cho, Kyunghyun and Birch, Alexandra and Haddow, Barry and Hitschler, Julian and Junczys-Dowmunt, Marcin and Läubli, Samuel and Miceli Barone, Antonio Valerio and Mokry, Jozef and Nadejde, Maria 2017. *Nematus: a Toolkit for Neural Machine Translation*, Proceedings of the Software Demonstrations of the 15th Conference of the European Chapter of the Association for Computational Linguistics 65–68 Association for Computational Linguistics

Sutskever, Ilya and Vinyals, Oriol and Le, Quoc V 2014. *Sequence to sequence learning with neural networks*, Advances in neural information processing systems 3104–3112

Turchi, Marco and De Bie, Tijl and Cristianini, Nello 2008. Alternation. *Learning performance of a machine translation system: a statistical and computational analysis*, Proceedings of the Third Workshop on Statistical Machine Translation 35–43 Association for Computational Linguistics

Vaswani, Ashish and Shazeer, Noam and Parmar, Niki and Uszkoreit, Jakob and Jones, Llion and Gomez, Aidan N and Kaiser, Łukasz and Polosukhin, Illia 2017. *Attention is all you need*, Advances in neural information processing systems 5998–6008

Factored Neural Machine Translation at LoResMT 2019

Saptarashmi Bandyopadhyay
Department of Computer Science and Engineering
Pennsylvania State University, University Park
University Park, P.A., U.S.A.
sbandyo20@gmail.com

Abstract

Low resource languages face a major challenge in developing machine translation systems due to unavailability of accurate and parallel datasets with a large corpus size. In the present work, Factored Neural machine Translation Systems have been developed for the following bidirectional language pairs: English & Bhojpuri, English & Magahi, English & Sindhi along with the uni-directional language pair English - Latvian. Both the lemma and Part of Speech (PoS) tags are included as factors to the surface-level English words. No factoring has been done on the low resource language side. The submitted systems have been developed with the parallel datasets provided and no additional parallel or monolingual data have been included. All the seven systems have been evaluated by the LoResMT 2019 organizers in terms of BLEU score, Precision, Recall and F-measure evaluation metrics. It is observed that better evaluation scores have been obtained in those MT systems in which English is the target language. The reason behind this is that the incorporation of lemma and pos tags factors for English words has improved the vocabulary coverage and has also helped in generalization. It is expected that incorporation of linguistic factors on the low resource language words would have improved the evaluation scores of the MT systems involving those languages on the target side.

1 Introduction

Data driven machine translation systems do not perform well involving Low Resource (LowRes languages since less parallel data are publicly available for these languages. However, limited monolingual data along with language analysis tools with acceptable performance measures are available for such languages. Incidentally, a large number of people use such low resource languages.

Neural machine translation (NMT) systems are the current state-of-the-art systems as the translation accuracy of such systems is very high for languages with large amount of training corpora being available publicly. Current NMT Systems that deal with LowRes languages (Guzman et. al., 2019; AMTA, 2018) are based on unsupervised neural machine translation, semi-supervised neural machine translation, pretraining methods leveraging monolingual data and multilingual neural machine translation among others.

Meanwhile, research work on Factored NMT systems (Koehn and Knowles, 2017; Garcia-Martinez et. al. 2016; Senrich and Haddow, 2016) have evolved over the years. The factored NMT architecture has played a significant role in increasing the vocabulary coverage over standard NMT systems. The syntactic and semantic information from the language is useful to generalize the neural models being learnt from the parallel corpora. The number of unknown words also decreases in Factored NMT systems.

In the present work, the idea of using factored neural machine translation has been explored in the 7 machine translation systems. The parallel corpus has been augmented to include factors like Lemma (using Porter Stemmer) and PoS tags (using TnT Tagger) for English words. No factoring has been done on the low resource language side. After factoring is done, the training dataset has been tokenized and byte pair encoding has been implemented, thereafter.

2   Related Works

The major research areas in low resource MT systems are described in (Guzman et. al., 2019; AMTA, 2018). One major area of research is to effectively use available monolingual data. It includes semi-supervised methods relying on backtranslation, integration of a language model into the decoder extending to unsupervised approaches that use monolingual data both for learning good language models and for creating artificial parallel data.

Another primary area of research is to work on a weakly supervised learning setup in which original parallel training corpus is augmented with comparable corpora. NMT systems for low resource languages have been developed in (Guzman et. al., 2019; AMTA, 2018) in four learning settings, semi-supervised in which monolingual data is utilized on the target side, weakly supervised setting in which noisy comparable corpora is used, fully unsupervised setting in which only monolingual data on both the source and the target sides are used to train the model and the supervised model in which only parallel corpus is used during training.

The vocabulary coverage increases significantly in factored neural architecture (Koehn and Knowles, 2017; Garcia-Martinez et. al.. 2016; Senrich and Haddow, 2016) while decreasing the number of unknown words. The linguistic decomposition of the words in terms of factors like lemma, PoS tags and other grammatical information can be applied on the source or on the target side or on both the sides.

According to the literature survey factored NMT system has not yet been applied to MT system development in Low Resource languages.

3   Factored Neural Machine Translation System

The following language pairs have been considered for development of Factored Neural Machine Translation systems:
1) English to Bhojpuri
2) Bhojpuri to English
3) English to Magahi
4) Magahi to English
5) English to Sindhi
6) Sindhi to English
7) English to Latvian

Only the provided corpora has been used for translation in all cases. The English side of the parallel corpora has been factored with the lemma and Part-of-Speech(PoS) tag of the surface word in all the 7 language pairs. The English lemma has been obtained using the Porter Stemmer (Porter, 1980). The TnT tagger has been used to obtain the PoS tags of English words (Brants, 2000). An example is as follows: the factor information of the surface word 'When' is obtained and augmented as 'When|when|WRB', where 'when' is the lemma and 'WRB' or 'Wh-adverb' is the PoS tag for the surface-level English word 'When'. No factoring has been done for the low resource language (Bhojpuri, Magahi, Sindhi, Latvian) side of the parallel corpora. Then the model for byte pair encoding (BPE) is trained with the training corpus on the source and target sides for all the language pairs. The vocabulary for byte pair encoding (BPE) is constructed with 32000 vocabulary size. Pre-tokenization has not been done as sentencepiece[1] tool has been used which does not always require pre-tokenization. The source and the target sides of the parallel corpora are then encoded using the model constructed by sentencepiece[1]. These datasets are used for training the neural model for translation. The parameters for training the neural model for translation for each of the language pairs are:
i)   Drop-out rate = 0.3
ii) 2 layered unidirectional recurrent neural network with Long Short Term Memory (LSTM) as the recurrent unit
iii) Batch size = 128 and 500 hidden units
iv) 14000 training steps
v)   Beam search as inference mode with a beam width of 5 and a length penalty weight and a coverage penalty weight of 0.4 each.

After the model is trained, the test dataset on the source side of the language pair is used to obtain the output dataset on the target side of the language pair. Once testing is done, the data is again decoded by sentencepiece[1] using the trained BPE model before. Thus, Method1 is achieved for language pairs where the low resource language is on the target side. When English is on the target side of the language pair, the generated dataset is subjected to post-processing to remove the factored information of lemma and PoS tag in it. This is referred to as Method1 for language pairs where English is on the target side. Method2 is a slight modification of Method1 where the space before punctuations ('.',',',';',':','"','' and '!') are removed in case of language pairs where English is on the target side. For 3 low resource languages,

----

[1]https://github.com/google/sentencepiece

Bhojpuri, Magahi, and Sindhi, the spaced before certain punctuation marks ('|' and '!') are removed in order to study the impact of the punctuations on the BLEU scores. This is called Method2 for language pairs where the low-resource languages Bhojpuri, Sindhi and Magahi are on the target side.

4 System Evaluation Results

The results for the 7 language pairs have been illustrated in this section. It has been observed that Method 1 and Method 2 are leading to the same BLEU score, precision, recall and F-measure scores. It implies that the removal of the space character before certain punctuation marks do not have any effect on the Bleu score. Hence, the method column in the subsequent result tables have not been mentioned. The result of the Best Team for the specific language pair has been included. Since, no details are available about the specific method used by the Best team, no direct comparison has been made.

Team	BLEU score	Precision	Recall	F-measure
My Team (L19T6)	6.83	11.73	11.59	11.6
Best Team (L19T2)	10.69	16.74	17.07	16.9

Table 1: English-Bhojpuri FNMT System Results

The BLEU score for English-Bhojpuri language pair has been the second best among all the submissions. The Bleu score of the submitted system is 36% below the Best Team Score.

The Bhojpuri to English language pair also exhibits a good performance in the BLEU score. It is observed that higher Bleu scores are obtained with English as the target language. The Bleu score of the submitted system is 21% less than the Best Team Score. The precision score is only 6.5% less than that of the Best Team.

Team	BLEU score	Precision	Recall	F-measure
My Team (L19T6)	13.39	20.84	17.41	18.99
Best Team (L19T2)	17.03	22.28	22.43	22.35

Table 2: Bhojpuri-English FNMT System Results

The Bleu score for English-Sindhi submitted system is 59% lower than the Best Team System score, as shown in Table 3.

Team	BLEU score	Precision	Recall	F-measure
My Team (L19T6)	15.34	21.02	20.26	20.63
Best Team (L19T2)	37.58	40.4	40.52	40.46

Table 3: English-Sindhi FNMT System Results

Team	BLEU score	Precision	Recall	F-measure
My Team (L19T6)	26.2	33.24	29.54	31.28
Best Team (L19T2)	31.32	36.06	35.86	35.96

Table 4:Sindhi-English FNMT System Results

The Sindhi to English language pair also exhibits a good performance in the BLEU score. It is observed that higher Bleu scores are obtained with English as the target language. The Bleu score of L19T6 is 16% less than the Best Team Score.

Team	BLEU score	Precision	Recall	F-measure
My Team (L19T6)	9.02	12.01	15.43	13.41
Best Team (L19T1)	48.88	51.09	51.19	51.14

Table 5:English-Latvian FNMT System Results

The Bleu score for English-Latvian submitted system is 82% lower than the Best Team System score. It demonstrates that simply using the parallel corpus in the MT system does not always provide better result.

Team	BLEU score	Preci-sion	Re-call	F-meas-ure
My Team (L19T6)	0.24	5.82	3.48	4.36
Best Team (L19T2)	9.37	16.21	17.06	16.62

Table 6: English-Magahi FNMT System Results

The performance of the English-Magahi is worse as the Bleu score of the submitted system is 97% below the Best Team score. However, the F-measure of the submitted system is 74% below the Best Team score. Thus, there is a better correlation with human judgment.

Team	BLEU score	Preci-sion	Re-call	F-meas-ure
My Team (L19T6)	0.13	3.91	2.5	3.05
Best Team (L19T2)	9.71	16.55	17.15	16.84

Table 7:Magahi-English FNMT System Results

The performance of the Magahi - English is similarly worse as the Bleu score of the submitted system is 98% below the Best Team score. However, the F-measure of the submitted system is 82% below the Best Team score. Thus the correlation with human judgment is comparatively higher.

5   Conclusion

Factored Neural Machine Translation systems have been developed for the following Bidirectional language pairs: English & Bhojpuri, English & Sindhi, English & Magahi and English-Latvian. All the languages except English are Low Resource languages in which accurate and parallel datasets with larger corpus size are not available. Both the lemma and POS tags are included as factors on the English words while no factoring has been done on the low resource language side. The submitted systems have been developed only with the parallel corpus provided. Analysis of the system evaluation results demonstrate that inclusion of the lemma and PoS tags as factors on the English target side improves the Bleu score than when English is on the source side. The translation quality for English-Bhojpuri and Bhojpuri-English language pairs is very good, without using any additional dataset and by using a standard neural architecture of a 2 layered un-directional recurrent neural network, to learn the language model for translation. The lower values of the Bleu scores for the submitted systems English-Latvian, English - Magahi and Magahi-English demonstrate that using the parallel corpus only in developing the FNMT system does not improve the system evaluation scores.

References

Francisco Guzman et. al.. 2019. Two New Evaluation Data-Sets for Low-Resource Machine Translation: Nepali–English and Sinhala–English. arXiv:1902.01382v1 [cs.CL].

AMTA. 2018. Workshop on Technologies for MT of Low Resource Languages (LoResMT 2018). *The 13th Conference of the Association for Machine Translation in the Americas.*

Phillip Koehn and Rebecca Knowles. 2017. Six Challenges for Neural Machine Translation, In *Proceedings of the First Workshop on Neural Machine Translation*, Vancouver, Canada, August 4, 28-39.

Mercedes Garcıa-Martınez et. al.. 2016. Factored Neural Machine Translation Architectures, In *Proceedings of IWSLT 2016.*

Rico Sennrich and Barry Haddow. 2016. Linguistic Input Features Improve Neural Machine Translation, In *Proceedings of the First Conference on Machine Translation*, Volume 1: Research Papers, Berlin, Germany, August 11-12, 83-91.

Thorsten Brants. 2000. TnT - A Statistical Part-of-Speech Tagger, In Proceedings of the sixth conference on Applied natural language processing, 224-231.

Porter, M. 1980. An algorithm for suffix stripping. *Program* (14.3): 130-137.

JHU LoResMT 2019 Shared Task System Description

Paul McNamee

Johns Hopkins University

Human Language Technology Center of Excellence

810 Wyman Park Dr., Baltimore, Maryland 21211 USA

mcnamee@jhu.edu

Abstract

We describe the JHU submission to the LoResMT 2019 shared task, which involved translating between Bhojpuri, Latvian, Magahi, and Sindhi, to and from English. JHU submitted runs for all eight language pairs. Baseline runs using phrase-based statistical machine translation (SMT) and neural machine translation (NMT) were produced. We also submitted neural runs that made use of backtranslation and ensembling. Preliminary results suggest that system performance is reasonable given the limited amount of training data.

1 Introduction

JHU submitted runs for each of the eight language pairs in the shared task. A goal of our participation was to compare baseline SMT and NMT systems in low resource conditions. For the most part we used homogenous processing for our runs involving different language pairs. However, our primary interest was exploring translation to English, and we paid more attention and submitted more runs for those conditions. Also, there was so little data for Magahi, that using different hyperparameters seemed well-motivated. We used monolingual English data in some of our submissions, but did not make use of the monolingual data provided in other languages. Our team code was L19T5.

2 Data

The amount of provided parallel data, by language, is shown in Table 1. Note, the provided Sindhi data

Pair	Train	Tune	Test
bho–eng	28,999	500	250
lav–eng	54,000	1,000	500
mag–eng	3,710	500	250
sin–eng	29,014	500	250

Table 1: Number of parallel sentences used for each language pair, by partition. Test sets with English as the source language had the same size, except for eng–sin which had a test set of 249 sentences.

was marked as "sin", however the ISO-639-3 code for Sindhi is "snd". We use "sin" throughout for consistency with the shared task.

3 Models

In this section we describe the methods used to produce submissions to the task. Where English was the source language we used a SMT baseline to produce one submission, and we used NMT to both produce a submission and to translate 100,000 English sentences to the source language for subsequent use in backtranslation experiments. Characteristics of the submissions are shown in Table 2 and Table 3.

3.1 SMT Baseline

A phrase-based SMT system, Apache Joshua (Post et al., 2015), was used for Condition A[1] and for Condition C[2]. Sentences were tokenized using the Moses tokenizer and lower-cased (when appropriate). Sentences longer than 75 tokens in length were ignored during training. KenLM (Heafield, 2011) was used to train 4–gram language models using the target side of training bitext. When translating to English, a larger language model based on

[1] Provided corpora only

[2] Use of publicly available corpora

Run	Cond	Type	Aux. LM	BPE units	Chkpt freq
L19T5-bho2eng-pbmt-a	A	SMT	–	–	–
L19T5-bho2eng-pbmtlm-a	C	SMT	Yes	–	–
L19T5-bho2eng-xform-a	A	NMT	–	10,000	4,000
L19T5-bho2eng-xformbt-a	C	NMT	–	15,000	4,000
L19T5-lav2eng-pbmt-a	A	SMT	–	–	–
L19T5-lav2eng-pbmtlm-a	C	SMT	Yes	–	–
L19T5-lav2eng-xform-a	A	NMT	–	10,000	4,000
L19T5-lav2eng-xformbt-a	C	NMT	–	15,000	4,000
L19T5-mag2eng-pbmt-a	A	SMT	–	–	–
L19T5-mag2eng-pbmtlm-a	C	SMT	Yes	–	–
L19T5-mag2eng-xform-a	A	NMT	–	2,500	2,000
L19T5-mag2eng-xformbt-a	C	NMT	–	15,000	4,000
L19T5-sin2eng-pbmt-a	A	SMT	–	–	–
L19T5-sin2eng-pbmtlm-a	C	SMT	Yes	–	–
L19T5-sin2eng-xform-a	A	NMT	–	10,000	4,000
L19T5-sin2eng-xformbt-a	C	NMT	–	15,000	4,000

Table 2: Characteristics of submitted runs with English as the target language. Note, the runs labelled "xformbt-a" were named in error — they were in fact Condition C runs.

Run	Cond	Type	Aux. LM	BPE units	Chkpt freq
L19T5-eng2bho-pbmt-a	A	SMT	–	–	–
L19T5-eng2bho-xform-a	A	NMT	–	10,000	4,000
L19T5-eng2lav-pbmt-a	A	SMT	–	–	–
L19T5-eng2lav-xform-a	A	NMT	–	10,000	4,000
L19T5-eng2mag-pbmt-a	A	SMT	–	–	–
L19T5-eng2mag-xform-a	A	NMT	–	2,500	2,000
L19T5-eng2sin-pbmt-a	A	SMT	–	–	–
L19T5-eng2sin-xform-a	A	NMT	–	10,000	4,000

Table 3: Characteristics of submitted runs with English as the source language.

a 5% sample of English Gigaword 5th edition[3] was also used (10.5 million sentences, 229 million tokens).

In Condition C, no additional bitext was utilized in any of the language pairs, however, a larger target-side language model was used for models translating to English.

3.2 NMT Baseline

The second system we employed was Sockeye (Hieber et al., 2017), a sequence-to-sequence transduction model based on the Apache MXNet library. Sockeye supports CNNs, RNNs, and Transformer models. For the LoResMT shared task we used transformer models (Vaswani et al., 2017). The models used 4 stacked layers in the encoder and decoder, an embedding and model size of 512, a feed-forward hidden layer size of 1024 units, and 8 self-attention heads. Training was done with a batch size of 4,096 words, a checkpoint frequency of either 2,000 or 4,000, and an initial learning rate of 0.0002. The optimizer was Adam. Training continued until validation perplexity failed to improve for 10 consecutive checkpoints, or until the maximal number of epochs (100) was reached. Initial models were trained for Condition A in both translation directions for all four low resource languages. Text was tokenized by the Moses tokenizer, lowercased, and then BPE was applied using 2,500 to 15,000 BPE units (Sennrich et al., 2016), depending on the language and condition.

The four NMT runs for the English-to-X pairs were based on training a single model in each language. However, four independently trained models with different random initializations were used to create ensemble decodes in the X-to-English pairs. Sockeye provides support for ensemble decoding by combining output layer probabilities from separate training instances.

3.3 NMT with Backtranslation

In Condition C we again used no additional bitext, however, these neural runs used 100,000 sentences randomly drawn from our English Gigaword subsample to create synthetic bitext using backtranslation with an English-to-X model used for Condition A. These machine-produced translations were then used with the provided bitext to build X-to-English models, and inference was again per-

---

[3]LDC2011T07

formed using an ensemble of four separate models. Our interest was in seeing whether backtranslation would provide gains in very low resource settings.

4 Results and Discussion

All of our runs with English as the source language were Condition A (*i.e.,* provided data only). Results for these runs are shown in Table 4. We observe that phrase-based MT outperformed neural MT in all four low-resource scenarios, which is not too surprising given the limited amount of provided training data (refer to Table 1).

Pair	SMT	NMT
eng–bho	**3.01**	1.00
eng–lav	**23.24**	13.22
eng–mag	**5.66**	1.74
eng–sin	**7.72**	3.08

Table 4: Baseline SMT (pbmt) and NMT (xform) runs where English was the source language. All runs are Condition A.

Results with English as the target language are shown in Table 5.

Pair	SMT	SMT+LM	NMT	NMT+BT
bho–eng	14.20	0.14	**15.19**	13.05
lav–eng	**36.93**	1.24	34.54	35.48
mag–eng	**5.64**	0.32	4.32	1.37
sin–eng	24.55	0.11	**28.85**	23.10

Table 5: Runs for four conditions when English was the target language: SMT Baseline (A), SMT w/ auxiliary LM (C), NMT Baseline (A), and NMT using backtranslation (C).

With English as the target language, the results are mixed. SMT outperforms in two of four languages, and NMT is better in the other two. The SMT runs that used an auxiliary language model failed utterly — the results appear so poor, that it seems possible that an error was made during processing.

We observe notably higher scores in Latvian, which makes sense as it is the language pair with the greatest amount of training bitext (54,000 sentences). However, Sindhi and Bhojpuri have training sets of comparable size, yet Sindhi has appreciably higher scores.

Our recipe for backtranslation failed in three of four cases. Only in the highest resource language (*i.e.,* Latvian) did we find higher BLEU scores in our NMT models when backtranslating English text.

5 Conclusion

We created baseline SMT and NMT systems for the LoResMT 2019 shared task, and our submitted runs appeared to perform relatively well based on the preliminary results released by the task organizers. While language model augmentation failed to improve SMT performance for as yet undetermined reasons, use of backtranslation was successful in the highest resource language setting. In general, the statistical models outperformed the neural models in these low resource settings, a finding consistent with other reports in the literature (Koehn and Knowles, 2017).

References

Heafield, Kenneth. 2011. Kenlm: Faster and smaller language model queries. In *Proceedings of the sixth workshop on statistical machine translation*, pages 187–197. Association for Computational Linguistics.

Hieber, Felix, Tobias Domhan, Michael Denkowski, David Vilar, Artem Sokolov, Ann Clifton, and Matt Post. 2017. Sockeye: A toolkit for neural machine translation. *CoRR*, abs/1712.05690.

Koehn, Philipp and Rebecca Knowles. 2017. Six challenges for neural machine translation. In *Proceedings of the First Workshop on Neural Machine Translation*, pages 28–39, Vancouver, August. Association for Computational Linguistics.

Post, Matt, Yuan Cao, and Gaurav Kumar. 2015. Joshua 6: A phrase-based and hierarchical statistical machine translation system. *The Prague Bulletin of Mathematical Linguistics*, 104(1):5–16.

Sennrich, Rico, Barry Haddow, and Alexandra Birch. 2016. Neural machine translation of rare words with subword units. In *Proceedings of the 54th Annual Meeting of the Association for Computational Linguistics (Volume 1: Long Papers)*, pages 1715–1725, Berlin, Germany, August. Association for Computational Linguistics.

Vaswani, Ashish, Noam Shazeer, Niki Parmar, Jakob Uszkoreit, Llion Jones, Aidan N Gomez, Ł ukasz Kaiser, and Illia Polosukhin. 2017. Attention is all you need. In Guyon, I., U. V. Luxburg, S. Bengio, H. Wallach, R. Fergus, S. Vishwanathan, and R. Garnett, editors, *Advances in Neural Information Processing Systems 30*, pages 5998–6008. Curran Associates, Inc.

Author Index

Association for Computational Linguistics
209 N. Eighth Street
Stroudsburg, Pennsylvania 18360

ISBN 978-1-5108-9246-0